Bone of Contention

Books in the Gina Mazzio RN Medical Series
Bone Dry
Sin & Bone
Bone Pit
Bone of Contention

Other novels by Bette Golden Lamb & J. J. Lamb
Sisters in Silence
Heir Today...

Books by J.J. Lamb - Zachariah Tobias Rolfe P.I. Series
A Nickel Jackpot
The Chinese Straight
Losers Take All
No Pat Hands

Bone of Contention

By
Bette Golden Lamb
&
J. J. Lamb

TWO BLACK SHEEP PRODUCTIONS
NOVATO CALIFORNIA

Bone of Contention
Copyright © 2014 by Bette Golden Lamb
& James J. Lamb

www.twoblacksheep.us

ISBN-13: 978-09851986-5-7
ISBN-10: 0-998511986-5-6

Cover Design: Kelly Cazzaniga
www.cazdesignstudio.com

Dedication

To Clifford Lamb (Mr. Pianoman) – a good person, a gifted musician, and a wonderful son.

Acknowledgments

A huge thank you, as always, to members of our wonderful critique group for their cogent comments and scrupulous editing – Margaret (Peggy) Lucke, Shelley Singer, Judith Yamamoto, and Nicola Trwst, plus our gratitude for the valuable input of Jenny Weber, RN; Jan Herr, MD; Rita Lakin (the title); and Kelly Cazzaniga, for coming to our rescue in the final moments of the third trimester.

Bette Golden Lamb & J. J. Lamb

Chapter 1

"Gimme a draft, will ya?"

Dominick Colletti slid onto a high stool in the small Bronx bar. He watched the bartender lift a clean mug, fill it, swipe away the excess foam with a spatula, and set it on the mahogany counter. When Dominick reached for it, the barkeep held onto the handle.

"Lay some cash on me, man."

"What the fuck …used to park my ass here every day … and now you don't trust me?"

"Don't matter. The boss don't like ex-cons … specially wife beaters. Can't say I do either. Pay up or get your ass moving."

Dominick glared at him, reached into his jeans, pulled out a crumpled twenty, and tossed it on the counter.

Remember you when you were a skinny-assed slime ball … used to sit next to me in home room. Big shot now, huh … filling beer mugs.

Dominick wanted to show the guy a thing or two, but he took in the broad shoulders and pumped-up delts and let it be.

The place was starting to fill up. Dominick recognized two of the men who came through the door and headed for a booth in the back. As they sat down, the waitress automatically set a couple of Genesee lagers on the table.

"Hey, Bobby, Cal!" Dominick laughed and grabbed his beer and worked his way through the standing drinkers toward the two men. "How's it hangin'?"

Bobby looked up at him. "I ain't got nothin' to say to you, loser."

"What's with the 'tude, man?"

1

Cal was silent, wouldn't look him in the eye. Dominick stood there watching Bobby take a long pull from his bottle. "You want it straight, Colletti?" Bobby said.

"Yeah ... I'm waitin'."

"Just how the hell a dumb fuck like you managed to grab onto a great gal like Gina Mazzio ... well, that don't figure. No way."

"Come on, Bobby, you know, it's a family thing. Mazzios and Collettis come from the same dumb village in the old country ... practically made the deal the day we were born. Besides," Dominick gave him a you-know-what snicker, "there ain't too many studs around like me."

"Yeah, some fuckin' stud. More like a prick. Beat up on your woman and damn-near kill her? You sure as hell are a piece of work."

"The bitch had it coming."

Bobby shot up from the seat. "Get your ass outta my sight and don't come back, Colletti, or I'll show you the kind of man you really are."

Cal popped up, stood by Bobby's side, said, "You got any sense, man, you'll turn tail and keep running. Vinnie Mazzio's looking for you."

"Yeah, so what?"

"I wouldn't want to mess with that ex-marine. He never was a pushover, and I think he has a few moves now you might not see coming."

"Yeah, yeah."

"You messed up his sister real bad," Cal said, sitting back down. "That kind of thing is gonna need settling. Ya hear?"

The room was silent; the crowd parted as Dominick walked back to his stool. He pointed to the bills and change on the bar and said to the barkeep, "Hit me."

"You ain't getting nothin' else, Colletti. Get your ass out of here ... no one wants to look at your ugly mug."

"Yeah?" Dominick slid to his feet, scooped up his money, and headed out. When he got to the door, he said back over his shoulder, "Well fuck you, too, you piece of shit."

He'd had it. Parole or no parole, he wasn't going to stay in New York and take all the shit everyone was tossing at him. It was time to find his ex-wife and finish what he'd started ... only this time he was going to do it so he didn't end up in the slammer.

Chapter 2

What started out as a fifteen-minute sprint had morphed into an intense workout for Gina and Harry. Like idiots, they'd dared each other into running up three steep hills that always gave them trouble even on their best days. Going up or going down made no difference to Gina – it left her breathless, with a body that was screaming: Stop!

Harry didn't look too good either.

She could barely lift her tired, cramping legs back up the stairs to their apartment. There was a time when this kind of workout would have left her only pleasantly tired, but right now she was really done in. All she wanted to do was fling herself across the sofa and flake out for the rest of the day.

Inside, Harry yanked off his sweat-soaked shorts and drenched tee shirt, hell-bent on racing her for the shower; in another minute he would be gone and she was too beat to even think about challenging him. She wiggled her toes in her sweaty Nikes and bent down to untie the laces.

The intercom to the front door buzzed through the apartment, over and over and over.

Someone's sitting on the damn thing.

"Who the hell can that be?" she shouted.

Harry turned around at the bathroom door and gave her one of his wicked grins. "Beats me, but I can't answer the door wearing nothing but a smile." He mooned her and disappeared into the shower.

"All right already," Gina muttered, untangling her shoelaces and pulling off her socks. "It's Saturday morning ... even the birds are still sleeping."

4

She padded barefoot out to the intercom, but before she could get there, the insistent buzzing started again.

"Okay, okay, okay!" She pressed the speaker button. "For God's sake, take your finger off that thing and tell me who you are."

"Flowers for Mazzio, Ms. Gina Mazzio."

The voice sounded weird, but familiar.

"Yeah, from whom?"

"From me, you dummy."

Her mind went blank for an instant, then she screamed, "Vinnie! Is that really you?"

"Who else would be abusing your doorbell this early in the morning?" her brother said.

"It's practically the crack of dawn, you idiot." She slammed her hand against the release button to buzz him in, then flung open the apartment door and zoomed down, all her pains and aches forgotten.

Vinnie was taking the steps two at a time; Gina met him halfway. "Come here you miserable brat." She flung herself into his arms and they hugged for a long moment. "Why didn't you tell me you were coming?"

"Now look what you've done," he said, ignoring her question. "You've crushed my flowers."

"What flowers?"

"The ones I meant to bring."

"Come on up, funny man. We have tons to catch up on. I haven't heard from you for over a week. I was starting to get antsy."

They strolled into the apartment arm-in-arm. Harry must have raced through his shower; he was waiting in the living room, tight wet curls framing his face, and only a towel tied around his middle. He was dripping wet, and so was the floor.

"Harry, Vinnie; Vinnie, Harry," Gina announced.

Harry thrust a hand out. "Hey man, it's great to finally meet you. Gina never stops talking about you."

"Hell, I have e-mails filled with Harry this, and Harry that. But if you really know Gina, you know she never stops talking."

"How about I make us some coffee," Gina said, "before you say one more word and end up with a knuckle sandwich." She moved toward the kitchen.

"No, no, stay and visit with your brother," Harry said. "I'll make the coffee." He cinched up his towel to keep it from slipping away. But instead of the kitchen, he headed for the bedroom. "Give me a sec to throw on some clothes. Be right there."

"Thought you told me you were re-upping for another tour," Gina said after Harry was gone. She sat down and patted the sofa next to her.

"Afghanistan's downsizing, so..."

"Something wrong, kid?"

"They offered me a way out, so I took it."

"A way out? That doesn't sound like the military." Gina looked closer at her brother. Her eye started to worry-twitch. There were dark circles under his eyes and his unhealthy pallor made her uneasy, plus he looked ten pounds lighter. "I can't tell you how happy that makes me. Happy I won't be waking up in the middle of the night obsessing about you."

Harry was back, rattling dishes in the kitchen, and soon the smell of fresh coffee wafted through the apartment.

"It was a medical discharge, sis."

Gina was confused; her heart hammered in her chest. "Why? Were you wounded?" She grabbed his hand. "Tell me what happened?"

6

Her brother's eyes grew large. One minute he was there with her, the next he had disappeared into some hidden valley deep inside.

"Just tell me," she said softly.

"I couldn't sleep anymore and I started to have hallucinations."

Harry set a cup of coffee on the table in front of Vinnie. "If you want me to leave, I'll understand."

Vinnie reached out and gulped down half the cup. "No, no. It doesn't matter … it is what it is."

Harry sat and Gina clutched her brother's hand, held it to her chest.

"You know, I had a bad feeling about re-upping." Vinnie said.

She was suddenly angry at Vinnie. Angry because she was worried, angry because she felt helpless, angry because her brother was in really deep, dark waters and could be swept away forever.

"For God's sake … then why did you go back again?" Gina couldn't stop herself from practically screaming at him. She was scared and she couldn't stand to see her brother in such pain. "What were you thinking?"

"Gina!" Harry said softly.

She bowed her head. "I'm sorry, I won't do that again."

Vinnie nodded, but he hadn't really reacted to anything. Words spilled from his mouth. "I guess I wasn't thinking." He reached out turned the cup handle first one way, then the other. "I knew I had no business signing on again."

"When I finished my first tour, I came home and there was no work for me. Nothing! God, I was so desperate. It seemed like me and a bunch of other ex-military types were fighting over the same job, along side of everyone else. There wasn't anything. I even tried hooking into a job at McDonald's. And you know, it wasn't some kid I was competing with … it was some guy or gal with little kids to feed. It was depressing. So I went back in. At least I'd have a paycheck, and I didn't much like being in the old neighborhood again anyway."

"Oh, Vinnie." A horrible sadness gripped Gina.

"Bad luck seemed to ride my tail from the day I hit Afghanistan. Our patrols turned into the same bloody exercise every day. Horrible things kept happening, like IEDs blowing up one vehicle after another. That's when I couldn't sleep anymore – all of it, all the bloody bodies would appear and reappear in my nightmares. Everything was being torn apart. It never ended."

"Man, that's hard to take," Harry said.

"It got so I spent most of my time thinking about taking my gun and swallowing a bullet. Get it over with once and for all."

"No, Vinnie. No!" Gina couldn't stop the tremors that rode her hands.

"And then I blew up."

"Blew up?"

"The three of us were out patrolling in our Humvee – you know, shooting the breeze while we bumped along a normal pothole-filled road. Afghanistan is pretty damn barren to start with, and we were in this area that was even more desolate. It was like being on the moon … like we'd left the planet. And it was so quiet out there. No one else in sight, no one shooting guns or missiles at us."

"What happened?" Gina was on the edge of her seat.

"I remember taking a really deep breath and thinking that maybe things were going to be okay. The three of us were cracking up, laughing at the stupid stuff you talk about with buddies."

"And?"

"We'd just had some chow and one of the guys told a dumb butt joke. The nineteen-year-old driver was laughing so hard he could barely catch his breath when his head blew up, splattered like an overripe melon all over me. No warning. Covered in my buddy's brains."

Gina's chest was shutting down. She could barely breathe.

"Man, I went nuts ... ballistic. I started shooting at everything, in every direction. I totally flipped out."

Everyone was silent for a long moment, Vinnie staring out into nowhere.

"Tell you what," Harry said quietly, "you sit back and relax while Gina and I fix us all some breakfast. Okay?"

"Sounds good."

* * *

Gina, Harry, and Vinnie sat around the small kitchen table, continuing to drink coffee. Vinnie kept folding, unfolding his paper napkin as though focusing on it would crystallize his thoughts, make sense of whatever was bothering him.

He'd only eaten some of his eggs and ignored the strips of bacon Gina had piled on his plate. The more she watched her brother, the more she could see how wound up he was, how unlike the baby brother she'd grown up with. The man she thought she knew.

"I'm sorry to lay all this on you," Vinnie said. "But hanging around the house with Mom and Dad hovering over me was making me crazier than I was when I got home. I had to get away."

"They can really get to you, even on the best of days." Gina stood and filled their cups with more coffee. "That was one of the reasons I left New York, too. Not the major reason, but one of them."

9

"Have you been getting any kind of help with this?" Harry said to Vinnie.

"Not really. I don't need those shrinks. Besides, I tried it. Like you're suggesting, I thought it would help. That's what everyone said."

"What happened?"

"I got tired of their thinking and rethinking every word I said. I knew I would be all right if I could just sleep again. If only I could shut it all down. I mean, I jump at every sound – whether it's a car backfiring or some kid yelling in the street." He started tearing his folded paper napkin into little squares, then gave that up and turned the squares into shredded nothings.

"It'll get better, Vinnie," Harry said, "but you need—"

"Why didn't you come to me?" Gina said. "I would have helped you find something. Harry and I could have been here for you."

"Listen, man," Harry said, "what do you want to do? What kind of work are you looking for?"

"I don't care what it is. I just want to feel useful … not like some loser."

When Gina looked into his eyes, she saw the naked fear she'd seen in dying patients. Tears gushed down his cheeks, a moment later his head fell to her shoulder. He whispered, "My head's bursting, sis. I can't take it anymore."

Harry laid a hand on his shoulder and squeezed hard. "Don't you worry about anything, man. We've got your back now."

Chapter 3

Dominick was really beat. Every muscle in his body was screaming at him after spending several days on a bus to get to San Francisco. He headed straight for the Tenderloin, a rundown neighborhood he'd heard about back East. He began to feel a lot better when he walked down the street.

Frisco, New York. It don't matter ... always a place to tuck your ass in a big city.

He'd squirreled away some cash during his three years in jail, and that hadn't been easy. But he'd done it. Called it his kill-stash. When he got out, he padded it by hitting up his ma for a big chunk of dough. Told her it was for getting a fresh start, but clammed up tight about how he was going away, leaving the state.

Couldn't tell her there's no starting something new 'til all the old fish got fried.

Besides, breaking parole was not exactly anything she'd buy into; there would have been no money coming his way. And his old man sure as hell wasn't gonna cough up any bread.

Right now, he needed to bed down and think. Do this right or it was back in the can, and he had no intention of ever doing time again.

He had to sidestep kids in torn jeans who were skateboarding on and off the sidewalk or dribbling basketballs. Walking from block to block, he stepped around out-and-out bums who were looking for handouts, and stepped over homeless drunks who spilled out from narrow doorways.

He found what he was looking for: another sign in the window of what looked like a three-story walkup. It was written on a sun-bleached piece of paper taped inside the glass: Room for Rent.

The building manager glared at him through the slim opening of a chained door.

"What do you want?"

"Hi, I'm new in town. Saw your sign."

The man unchained and half-opened the door. Piercing eyes searched Dominick's face, then blatantly looked him up and down, taking in all of Dominick's six-foot-two frame.

Dominick had seen that look too many times – the one that said he couldn't be trusted – it really yanked his chain. He clamped down a knee-jerk reaction to punch out the creep. This was the third *Vacancy* sign he'd checked out. None of the managers had been able to offer a half-decent room. Now it was getting late in the day. He couldn't afford another night in a hotel, even in this rundown part of town. Besides, he wasn't taking any chances on getting pulled in by some nosy cop.

Dominick gave the man the once over. Even though the super was a short guy, he looked like a powerhouse, with overly pumped up arm muscles.

Jeez, is there anyone who doesn't hit the gym anymore?

Three years in prison and doing his daily workouts had toughened Dominick, but the temper that had gotten him in trouble in the first place never seemed to cool down. Prison did teach him to mask his kill response with a silly-assed grin. That usually shut off the alarm in most people, even the cons he hung out with in the yard.

The manager finally said, "Just because I have a vacancy doesn't mean *you* get to fill it."

"Hey, I just arrived in Frisco and I really need a place to bed down. I'd appreciate it if I could take a quick look."

The manager's eyes didn't let up; his gaze, long and hard, continued to punch holes in Dominick's head and body – it was starting to burn.

Finally, "All right then, Mr. ..."

"Colletti ... Dominick Colletti."

"I'll take you up and you can decide."

* * *

Dominic threw his duffel on the single bed. The mattress was lumpy and smelled rank even though it looked fairly clean. He opened the bag and scooped out jeans, underwear, and tees, which he stashed in a small press-board dresser that also smelled a bit rank. He hung up his two new colorless and boring sport shirts – they didn't flash the kind of look he usually shot for – and shoved them into a tiny closet. Too bad there was no bathroom in his room; he'd have to use the one down the hall. He hadn't checked it out yet, but he already knew what it would look and smell like.

He paced the room, then raised the yellowed shade and looked out at the street below. Panhandlers were busy hustling people and fog was moving in from the ocean. After a moment or two, his eyes grew heavy. Even though it was too early to hit the sack, he needed to get some shut-eye. He was beat.

He untied his shoes and kicked them off; they flew across the room. He emptied the rest of the duffel on the bed. All that was left was a small corkboard target and a handful of darts wrapped in a wash cloth and held together with two loops of a rubber band.

Smiling, he hung the corkboard on the back of the door, then unwrapped the darts and placed them on the dresser.

He stretched up and reached out, tensed and relaxed his arm muscles, and moved his head from side to side. Then in one sudden motion he spun around, grabbed a dart, and threw it at

13

the board. It thumped hard and dug in right between the eyes of a pasted-on photo of Gina, his ex-wife.

Chapter 4

Gina hesitated before taking the final step that would carry her through the automated doors of Ridgewood Hospital's main entrance. Memories crowded around her.

Had it only been two months since she'd worked here and got that crazy stop-him-before–he–kills-again telephone call?

And it seemed more like forever since Harry talked her into taking a leave of absence, and joining him for something different and, hopefully, more restful: her first travel nurse assignment.

That hadn't worked out so well going into the isolated wilds of Nevada. At first the assignment had sounded like an adventure, but they soon found out they'd been suckered into a medical nightmare. She and Harry had been lucky to make it out alive.

And she'd thought growing up in the Bronx was tough.

Was there any place on the planet that was safe for her ... for anyone? Maybe she yearned for the impossible. Instead of a dependable, consistent sameness, life was always going to be a roller coaster.

And could a person be wise and stupid at the same time?

Well, bring on the fog. It was good to be back in San Francisco with the Golden Gate Bridge and bay waters. The weather had turned cooler than usual for October. She wore a pair of charcoal wool slacks, a burgundy turtleneck, and a black tailored jacket – warm enough, but much more formal than her daily garb. If she hadn't had an appointment with Alan Vasquez, Ridgewood's administrator, she'd have worn jeans and a running jacket. And if she'd been on duty, it would have been scrubs.

15

When she'd worked at Ridgewood before, she'd usually parked her temperamental red Fiat on one of the side streets adjoining the huge hospital complex, then zipped in through an auxiliary entrance near the ER. At six-thirty in the morning, she never really saw much of anyone other than security guards and medical personnel – people like her who were focused on getting to their work stations.

Today, at ten a.m., she was forced to squeeze the little Fiat into a space that left miniscule gaps between the cars parked in front and behind her. It was an arm-wrenching struggle, but she refused to park in the underground tomb Ridgewood called a garage. She had an unreasonable fear that her car would be ingested by a metal-chomping SUV.

Walking leisurely through the hospital atrium, she stepped through the sliding glass doors into the main building – but not fast enough for some people, who seemed to bump into her intentionally to push her forward. It was crowded inside and she could see medical problems all around her – people on crutches and in wheel chairs. Many with that brave veneer of false normalcy that told her they were swallowing back pain, or pain pills, just to keep going.

She took a deep breath and glanced at her watch as she stepped into the elevator. She pressed the button for the top floor – Administration – and was pleased that she would be right on time.

* * *

Alan Vasquez stood up and walked around the desk the moment Gina entered his office. Gina remembered that once there had been so much animosity between them, he never would have seen her without a union rep or nursing supervisor present. That is, if she got to see him at all. But events in his personal life had changed everything.

Gina had been instrumental in finding out what happened to Arina Diaz, his niece and her friend. The results had not been good, but it had changed their relationship. She still didn't like administrators, but Vasquez was a different person now, and things had become honest and amicable between them. They'd learned to respect each other. "How are you, Ms. Mazzio?" he said, taking her hand. "I was surprised, but pleased, to hear that you'll be coming back to work for us next week."

"It's a big surprise to me, too."

Vasquez's eyebrow shot up, questioning her. "Oh?"

"It's a long story, but let's just say Nevada is never going to make it for me."

"Have a seat," he said. "What can I do for you?"

Gina slipped into a comfortable leather chair opposite Vasquez, who sat down behind his desk. Maybe it was her imagination but his office seemed more comfortable and less business-like than the last time she was here. For one thing, a large bouquet of bright lavender mums spread magnificently in a crystal vase at the end of his desk next to a picture of his deceased niece. His eyes followed Gina's and his face paled.

"I miss Arina more than I can say."

Gina nodded and had to force her thoughts away from her murdered friend. "Mr. Vasquez, I have a favor to ask of you."

For just a flicker, his eyes narrowed, turned suspicious, but his inner dialogue must have overruled whatever thoughts he was having. "What is it?"

"My brother Vinnie came back about a week ago from a tour in Afghanistan and he needs a job."

"Not another Bronxite?" He held a hand up. "Just joking." He leaned forward in his chair. "Was he in the Medical Corps?"

"No. Just a grunt, like most everyone else."

17

"So you're talking about a janitorial or nurse's aide position?"

Gina shrugged and held her hands out, palms up. "I was hoping for something a little more upscale." She'd heard about the hiring freeze in those positions and guessed what Vasquez was going to say before he said it.

"Right now we're not hiring additional nursing techs. That's all under union control and I can't interfere. You know that, Ms. Mazzio."

"Vinnie ... really needs something," Gina blurted. "I need it ... for him." Her eyes filled with tears that spilled down her cheeks. "He's had a horrific time in the military. He's burned out and he needs our help. Someone has to step up for him ... be in his corner. If we can't bring him back from the brink, he may be lost forever. Please ..."

She couldn't say another word. If she did, she would break down and sob like a lunatic.

Vasquez sat at his desk tapping a pen, clicking the nib in and out, in and out. Gina didn't dare look at him, didn't know what she would do if he turned her down.

"Where are you scheduled to start work next week?"

"I'm not sure; I'm supposed to find out later today. There was talk of sliding me into the out-patient women's clinic."

"Mmmm. I see. Good, good." He continued to click his pen.

Chapter 5

The three of them sat at a small round table in Rosario's, Gina and Harry's favorite local trattoria. She loved the environment, thought it was almost like being in an open cave, but instead of moss covering the walls, there were dark wooden shelves loaded with all kinds of wines from the provinces in Italy.

She studied the features of her younger brother – dark curly hair, dark eyes, and cheekbones that were high and sculpted, not much different from her own. She couldn't help but compare him to the many Roman busts she'd seen in museums, even more so with his weight loss.

He'd never been easy to deal with, especially when he was a bratty kid and a huge pain in the neck to six-years-older Gina. This grown-up version looked to be even more of a challenge, particularly since he was now a couple of inches taller than her five-foot-ten.

But she loved him and she'd take him anyway she could get him, grateful he'd come back from the war zone alive. If only things would improve then she wouldn't feel so helpless watching him struggle to get through every day and night. Nighttime was the worst; he was plagued by nightmares that woke her and Harry, and probably all of their neighbors.

Gina wanted to believe that after a week she would really see he was getting better, and see *some* subtle signs of improvement. At least home cooking was filling him out and his energy level had picked up enough that he'd started to go on longer runs with the two of them.

The waiter set down a large platter filled with bruschettas. Gina and Harry reached for the same piece of garlicky tomato and grilled bread, but she was a micro second quicker. She gave him a winning smile before she took her first bite.

"I can't live with you guys too much longer," Vinnie said, taking a sip of the house red wine. "You're driving me nuts. I've got to get a place of my own."

"Apartments are really expensive in San Francisco," Harry said. "And we like having you around to pick on."

Vinnie's gaze bit into Harry, shoulders stiffened, jaw clenched. He looked like he was going to fly across the table and hit him.

Gina kneed her brother. "Oh come on, Vin. He's only pulling your leg. Get with it!"

After a moment, Vinnie visibly relaxed. "Sorry, Harry."

"Hey, man. It's nothing."

"God, I hate this. I can't seem to climb out of this hole I'm in."

"Give yourself a break, man. It's going to take time."

"Number one, you are *not* moving out." Gina reached for his arm and squeezed. "Like Harry said, it's expensive to live in San Francisco; you need some time without having to think about money. Maybe after you've worked a while at Ridgewood."

"Sometimes I really worry about you, Gina. I don't know where your head is. I keep telling you, I don't know squat about taking care of patients. Right now the idea of being responsible for somebody else scares me to death."

She smiled at him. "You may be stupid, but you're not dumb."

"You'll learn," Harry said. "And Internal Meds is a great place to start." He leaned over and gave Gina a kiss on the cheek. "Your sis has alerted some of her friends that work there ... they've agreed to make sure you have a smooth ride."

I can see why Gina loves you ... you're blind as a bat ... can't seem to see what a nut case she is. And will you stop kissing her all the time. I feel like a chaperone."

"Look, Vin, people are just people," Harry said. "Be yourself."

"Yeah, well, that's what I'm afraid of."

Gina grabbed his hand. "After the first day, you'll wonder why you even thought twice about it. You wanted to feel useful? Taking care of sick people will give you a whole new perspective, not only on the people who need you ... but of yourself."

Chapter 6

The next morning, Harry was too jumpy to hang around doing nothing; he'd gone straight to his assignment in ICU. Gina and Vinnie were sitting in the Ridgewood cafeteria, her first day back and Vinnie's first day on the job. They were waiting until it was time to go to work and Gina could see that her brother was nervous. She worried that he might not stay long enough to even make it up to his assigned unit.

The place was crowded, mostly with medical personnel getting ready for the day shift. Gina loved the cafeteria, with its loud, happy buzz of conversation, even though it was early enough that she could have easily gone home and crawled back into bed.

They had about ten minutes to kill before Gina was off to the Women's Health clinic and Vinnie went up to Internal Meds.

She could see it had been a bad mistake to bring him to the cafeteria. The clamor of the early morning laughing personnel all around them was starting to get to him. Watching him jump at sudden noises made her heart wrench. His reactions were worrisome—eyes darted here, there, everywhere; one foot tapped out a harsh, non-rhythmic beat under the table. The combination went all the way back to when he was a kid—just before he was about to do explode over something he'd held in for a long time.

She wanted to say something, anything to reassure him. But this Vinnie was very different from the brother she'd grown up with. More than anything, she didn't want to say the wrong thing and make it worse.

She was about to speak when Vinnie's eyes lit up and settled onto her friend Helen, who was wending her way to their table.

The petite Oncology nurse plopped down into a vacant chair next to Vinnie. "Welcome back, Gina. I knew the high desert was no place for you." Before Gina could answer, Helen turned her head toward Vinnie and nodded approvingly. "So this is the brother you're always talking about?"

"Yeah, meet my baby brother, Vinnie."

"Cut it out, will ya, sis?" But there was no anger in the response. His attention was totally fixed on Helen as he held out a hand.

Gina watched Helen reach for Vinnie's hand. When they touched, Gina could swear some kind of electricity passed between them.

Helen, who was never at a loss for some smart ass response, was very quiet as she held onto Vinnie's hand. How two people could become so wrapped up in each other in a single instant was remarkable – Gina could almost hear them breathing as one.

"Pleased to meet you," Helen finally said. "I ... I..."

"Me, too."

"Vinnie is starting in Internal Meds today. There are no classes for newbies because of the hiring freeze, so the floor nurses will be teaching him the skills he'll need to be a patient-care tech."

"Mmmm, how did you manage to pull that off?" Helen said to Gina. She gently pulled her hand away from Vinnie.

"Vasquez came through. He made it happen with a special dispensation through a veteran's organization. The union went for it."

Helen, in a soothing voice, said to Vinnie, "Don't worry about the job ... it being new and all. Those guys and gals will teach you what you need to know, pronto."

Vinnie smiled, but said nothing.

"Hey," Helen said, "I can tell you'll be great."

For the first time since he'd found out about the job, Gina thought her brother seemed almost calm. Somehow, Helen had wrapped an aura of confidence around him, just as she'd done for Gina so many times. But this was very, very different. Gina glanced at her watch, hating to break the spell that had sprung up to surround Helen and her brother.

"Well, we better get moving, Vin. This is going to be an interesting day, kid."

The three of them stood.

"I'll take him up to the floor and introduce him," Helen said. "It's on my way."

Gina reached out and placed a hand on his shoulder. "Give me a call later, let me know how it's going."

He gave her a wide smile. "I'll do that."

* * *

Dominick stared at his cell phone. He'd been trying to work up the courage to call his parents for the last ten minutes. In agitation, he'd paced around his room, thrown darts at Gina's picture, until he couldn't stand the tension anymore.

He'd been in Frisco a week now and had accomplished nothing. He still hadn't found Gina and he was at a dead end. The city was just too big with too many hospitals to scout out, to find the bitch. And it wasn't because he hadn't tried. He'd only gone to a couple when he realized there was no way he could cover all the shifts, all the entrances, all the ... everything.

24

It
was sickening. There were so many ins and outs of these big
buildings, she could disappear through one door while he was
still scanning another -- and he'd never know he missed her. It
was never going to work, unless he was *really* lucky.

Yeah, and his luck hadn't been so good lately.

Man, he didn't want to do this, didn't want to call home, but
he needed to stop spinning his wheels. His money was going
down the drain, some on rent, some on food. Mainly, he
couldn't stop popping into bars and drinking– and there were
plenty of bars in the Tenderloin. If this kept up, he'd have to get
some kind of gig to make some change for his pocket to cover
day-to-day living expenses.

He grabbed his cell and punched in his parents' number.

The phone rang and rang. All kinds of possible situations,
possible lies were racing through his head –none of them good
enough, especially if his mother answered.

No answer. He breathed a sigh of relief and was about to
disconnect when his mother's voice came on the other end.

"Ye-e-es."

"Hi Mom."

She immediately started screaming at him. "What'sa matter
with you? You take-a my money and leave-a town. You're an
idiot. Capisce?"

"Yes, mom."

"If it wasn't for your sister I would-a thought you dead. At
least you talk-a to her. No respect … lie to your own-a mama."

"I'm sorry mom. I'm really sorry."

"Your parole man, he call, say you gonna go back to prison
when they find you. Capisce? Back to jail!"

"Please don't tell them I'm in California."

"Why-a you there?"

"I came to apologize to Gina for what I did. I shouldn't have hurt her."

"So? Apologize, come-a home to the family."

"I'm having trouble finding her."

"At least Vinnie's a good boy. He call his mama, say he gonna work with Gina in the same-a hospital."

Know what I'd like to do with that "good boy." If I ever see the little prick, I'll break his neck. A fuckin' soldier. Who cares?

"Vinnie's out here in California?" Dominick held his breath. "So, what's the name of the place?"

He grabbed up a dart and threw it. It hit Gina's picture, stabbed her right between the eyes.

Chapter 7

Elyse Kyser lay shivering on her bed. She was naked under the sheets, covered in sweat; the linen had turned clammy and sticky.

Every morning for the past month she'd tried to swallow back the waves of nausea that wouldn't stop crawling up her throat, but she couldn't stop them. She pushed herself up and ran to the bathroom, barely making it in time.

The dry heaves and gagging that followed were even worse than the vomiting. She reached out for a washcloth, soaked it with cool water, and pressed it against her forehead to calm the spasms – it was the only thing that seemed to work. She squeezed the cloth and dribbled the moisture down her face, across her breasts, and onto to her belly and thighs.

Tears gushed; she couldn't stop sobbing.

I've always been so careful. How could this happen to me?

She walked on unsteady feet back to her bed and stretched out, arms over her head, hands resting on the pillow. She looked up at a colorful butterfly mobile hanging from the ceiling.

It looked so innocent.

The structure drifted one way, then the other. The room started spinning; she had to turn away.

This was the third day she'd had to call in sick.

I've already missed two periods. I have to make a decision, do something, and do it quickly.

Any more sick days and her cashier's job at Denny's would be out the window. The money barely covered the rent and her savings account was almost bottomed out.

Need to find a second job. Can I even study, stay in college with two jobs?

Her mind refused to settle down. She couldn't concentrate on present or future plans while her thoughts were filled with such self-hatred – how could she have been so stupid to go to bed with Thad?

Slowing her breathing, focusing on it, she soon realized how peaceful it was just to lie in bed following her breath.

In some strange way it made her feel translucent. Yes, that was the only word for it. Translucent.

When she closed her eyes she could see and feel every cell in her body float and fill with light. A new life was growing inside of her – she could visualize the frenzied cell division exploding in the embryo buried in the lining of her uterus. That thought consumed her every single day, from the moment she rose from the depths of sleep to the surface of complete awareness.

She looked at all the photographs hanging on the walls of her tiny apartment. Every bit of space was taken, each picture shoved right up against the next one. She particularly liked the one she'd recently purchased from Charlie Fortune – she'd barely had room to squeeze it in even after rearranging all the others. His series of what he called Ocean Flash haunted her. In this picture, he'd captured that single moment when a powerful ocean wave rose up and majestically hung in space before collapsing back into the vastness of an endless sea.

She couldn't afford any of these photographs, but she'd had to have them. Like the night she thought she had to have Thad, even though she'd forgotten to take the pill that morning. His lies made her feel beautiful, but he'd used her flesh, then told her it was only a one-night stand. That, right after they'd had sex. And true to his word, he'd ignored her in their Ocean Science class ever since.

What had she seen in him anyway?

That's what I get for taking a night off from studying and going out with some classmates for drinks. Doing something I shouldn't have been doing.

That's how I always get into trouble.

Desperate thoughts flashed through her head.

What am I going to do?

My parents will kill me if they find out.

I can't raise a child alone. I can barely take care of myself.

One lousy missed pill and I get caught.

Elyse got dressed. She opened her bedside table and pulled out a package of crackers she kept stored next to her iPad. The paper crackled as she opened it and pulled out a cracker; she took a deep breath when it managed to stay down. She swallowed a few sips of bottled water and looked up the address for Planned Parenthood. She had heard how helpful they could be. Maybe if she could talk to a counselor she wouldn't feel so alone, so frightened.

She forced herself to get dressed, gathered her backpack, purse, and was out the door.

* * *

When Elyse arrived at the small, two-story building, there was a large crowd of people parading in front carrying placards showing pictures of dead fetuses. The men and women carrying the signs were yelling at anyone who dared to walk past them into the clinic.

Elyse edged toward the entrance, but her legs refused to move any farther. She stood paralyzed, not knowing whether to walk on into the building, or leave.

One of the jeering men separated himself from the group. Without hesitation, he singled her out, hurried up to her, holding a sign imploring God to save her soul – he held it out and shook it like a rattle in front of him.

"You murdering whore," he screamed, inches from her face. "I would throw you in prison and let you rot." Spittle splattered her cheeks. "You will be punished!"

One of the others grabbed his elbow. "Marvin, stop it. Don't do this!" Marvin resisted, but was ultimately yanked away.

A news team was standing at the edge of the crowd, waiting for any sign of trouble so they could capture it on camera; they started to move in Elyse's direction.

Shaking, she turned away and hurried back to the bus stop.

Chapter 8

Gina didn't know whether to be thrilled or annoyed. She'd envisioned taking Vinnie to Internal Meds and introducing him to the nurses.

He's my brother, after all. Helen just snatched him away.

Gina hated that petty, mean side of her, the part that oozed out when she least expected it.

You want your brother to be happy, don't you?

His eyes hadn't lit up like that since he'd arrived in San Francisco. It was almost magical the way he and Helen had clicked.

That really surprised Gina. Helen was not too fond of the male sex – she'd been crushed in too many relationships. Was it the vulnerability written all over Vinnie's face?

Maybe this was what they both needed.

Gina walked slowly to the overpass that connected the main hospital and the clinics. She had hoped to find a spot in the Oncology Unit when she returned from Nevada, but the only openings were in the Outpatient clinics. At least she didn't have to go back to Telephone Advice where she'd taken a call that had gotten her into all sorts of trouble. Who would have thought talking on the telephone could be so dangerous?

Well, that was in the past. Now she would be working in the Outpatient Ob/Gyn clinic in a different capacity. At least it was a service she really enjoyed.

She was a few minutes early, but when she walked down the hallway to the Woman's Health unit, Darcy Yamashita, the manager, was waiting for her.

"Hi, Gina." She was wearing her name tag on her spotless white coat, and gave Gina a firm handshake.

Darcy was somewhere in her fifties, and Gina had liked her instantly when she'd been interviewed by her for the position; she seemed like a very warm and direct person.

"Welcome to our group. Come on, I'll show you around."

They walked through the Ob/Gyn waiting room. "This area was recently renovated," Darcy said. "Believe it or not, they even asked us to pick out our own colors. What do you think?"

"It's quite nice."

The walls were a soft green and there was no particular format or theme to the displayed art. Abstract and representational paintings hung side by side. It was obvious that all the chairs were newly upholstered in a pattern of dark green and coral geometrical designs. It felt cheerful.

As they walked down the hallways, the personnel they passed smiled at them. Darcy greeted most of them by their first names, and made introductions to several nurses and the janitor, who was vacuuming the floors.

Gina began to relax. Things were looking good.

"This wing is mostly devoted to prenatal care," Darcy said.

"Do you do your own high-risk screening?"

"Yes, and the routine high-risk prenatal care and counseling."

"Who follows those patients?"

"Mostly the NPs, but there're a few MDs involved. You won't be working in this wing. You're scheduled for Family Planning and Diagnostics."

Even though Gina had worked the telephones in Ridgewood's Ob/Gyn Advice Center, these clinics were a whole other universe. She felt a rush of excitement – direct relationships with people was why she had gone into nursing.

They turned into another wing and immediately came to a bold sign.

Procedures in Progress. Please Lower Your Voice

Gina gave the manager a questioning look.

Darcy seemed embarrassed. "There have been a number of complaints about the noise level in the corridors," she said. "I guess if you were having an abortion, you might complain about people laughing and carrying on outside your door."

"Do you do many therapeutic abortions in the clinic?"

"Quite a few TABs. People like the anonymity of coming to clinics that have all kinds of medical services other than just birth control and abortions," Darcy said. "That way they're not singled out and subjected to protest groups that harass them outside places like Planned Parenthood. That kind of attention makes a lot of women feel even guiltier than they do already."

"I can understand that."

"Speaking of which," Darcy said, "you'll be expected to rotate with two other nurses to assist with TABS and diagnostic procedures, along with three medical assistants."

"What kind of diagnostics are you referring to?"

"The standard treatments for fibroid problems: uterine artery embolization for one, or endometrial ablation for bleeding problems. You know," Darcy said, "the usual garden variety that goes along with an Ob/Gyn practice."

She pointed to the nurses' station. "That's where the nurses hang out ... but of course, I don't need to tell you about that place."

"No, I've spent a lot of time in them."

A woman dressed in scrubs started to hurry past the two of them, but Darcy said, "Hang on a minute, Thelma. I want you to meet our new nurse, Gina Mazzio."

"Hi," Gina said, offering a hand to the woman. Thelma barely shook her hand. Her only other response was the hint of a smile.

33

"Thelma is one of our best medical assistants," Darcy continued. "She'll be a great help to you."

Darcy and Gina walked into the station, where two RNs were studying patient computer notes at a long desk under an overhanging counter. The nurses looked away from what they were doing and glanced up at the supervisor.

"Gina Mazzio, meet Taneka Gray, the unit team leader, and Carrie Donovan, currently our only other staff nurse."

"It's about time we got some more help," Carrie said, her voice quavering.

Gina noticed her eyes seemed glassy, too bright.

Does she have a fever?

"We're really glad to have you," Carrie said. "We've been drowning here." She shook Gina's hand and then picked up the antibacterial foam container on the desk. "Sorry, you know how it is."

Her hand was so hot.

"Oh, yeah," Gina said. "I practically bathe in the stuff."

Carrie's body language was off. She appeared sick to Gina. Her hands were trembling when she rubbed them together to absorb the puff of foam.

Something's definitely wrong.

"Welcome," Taneka said, friendly but reserved. The black woman had a beautiful smile, but it seemed that she had other things on her mind that probably had nothing to do with Gina.

"Why don't the two of you take over and introduce Gina to the unit and the rest of the personnel," the manager said. "She'll learn a lot more about how everything works from you." She raised a hand and wiggled it. "See you later, gang."

* * *

34

"Carrie seems ill," Gina said as she and Taneka wandered through the unit. Taneka hesitated before responding. "She hasn't felt well today." She paused, then added, "And that after just taking a few days off."

"Maybe she should go home."

Taneka laughed. "She'd better not. There's too much to do and not enough hands to do it."

"But if she's sick—"

"And this is the TAB room," Taneka said, as though she hadn't heard. They walked past a crash cart and into a small surgical suite.

Gina looked around. It wasn't exactly spacious, but there was room enough to do what had to be done. A counter with drawers and a row of cabinets above and below had labels pasted on all the outer surfaces to tell what supplies were hidden out of sight. The white Formica countertop had jars of the usual 4x4s, packaged syringes, solutions, applicators. Operating room lights hung over the table, and equipment stood ready to hook up, follow and record a patient's vital signs. An IV stand, sentinel-like, waited for someone to hang necessary fluids. Floor-to-ceiling cabinets were at the back of the room, and in the corner at the foot of the table was a TAB suction machine with all its tubing.

"As you can see," Taneka said, "it's all pretty much standard."

"What's in the cabinets over there?" Gina pointed to the back of the room.

"Literature ... all kinds. After-care instructions. Birth control info." Taneka laughed. "Also, extra pillows, a blanket ... whatever else needs to be stuffed out of the way."

"How many abortions do you do in a day?"

"Usually two or three, three times a week, depending on the available room status. Any more questions?"

"No. Like you said, all standard stuff."

"Okay," Taneka said. "Let's wander over to the Gyn procedure rooms."

* * *

It looked like a smooth, well-organized clinic. Gina mentally patted herself on the back for her luck in slipping into this job.

This is going to be great.

When they came to the nurses' station again, Carrie was sitting at the desk, her head in her hands. When she looked up, her eyes were wild, unfocused. She jerked up and clutched her chest. Gina and Taneka rushed and caught her as she started to fall to the floor.

"I knew there was something wrong," Gina said. "Carrie, can you talk, tell us what's going on?"

"My heart … it's racing … I can barely breathe." Carrie began to shake so hard they could hear her teeth chattering.

"We need to get her to the ER," Taneka said, grabbing a phone from the desk.

Gina grabbed Carrie, reached out to take her pulse.

"Get a gurney, Gina … and bring the portable oxygen tank with you on the way back." Then the nurse was rattling off a litany of Carrie's symptoms on the phone. "No! We can't wait. We'll bring her down."

As they raced down the hall with the gurney, Taneka was yelling, "Thelma! Thelma!"

* * *

Thelma Karsh hurried to respond. "I'm here," she called out. She watched the lead nurse and the new staff nurse stuff the gurney and themselves into the elevator.

"We're going to the ER," Taneka yelled at her.
"What happened?"
But the door slammed shut. Thelma couldn't help but smile.

Chapter 9

Thelma Karsh couldn't sit still – excitement was curling in her belly, pressing down on her; she almost peed her pants.

Smart-mouth Carrie was on the way to the ER. And *she,* Thelma, was the reason.

It had taken all of her self-control not to laugh at Taneka and that new nurse trying to maneuver the gurney into the elevator. They looked pretty funny, both of them huffing, their eyes wide with fear.

Carrie? Her face was white as virgin snow.

And that was the only virgin thing about her. Filthy whore! Murderer!

Thelma had listened to, tolerated Taneka fire off orders, telling her what to do. And she had nodded like a good drone because she wouldn't let on that she was way smarter than any of them thought.

When she'd started here three years ago she'd done what they told her, signed all the orientation documents, because to work in Woman's Health, she'd had to agree to assist with therapeutic abortions.

She hated herself for doing it.

If she hadn't needed the money, she would have torn up the papers and thrown them back in their faces. But she'd finally agreed for only one reason: she would make those baby murderers pay with their lives.

And now she had a big secret weapon.

So, yes, she would continue to do as she was told, be mild mannered, and cause Taneka to give her excellent performance evaluations so she could make even more money. But she would still do her real work. The work of God.

She fingered the gold cross that always hung around her neck – touching it made her feel strong, strong enough to be a good soldier.

For a long time she'd hesitated to do what she and Marvin had planned – get rid of women who murdered their growing babies.

"Do something real. Make a difference," Marvin had yelled, no screamed, at her when she hesitated to take action. "Wasn't that the reason you went to work for that killing machine?"

Then he started pushing her around. He'd shoved her into a table, broke her leg. And he continued to call her a weak soldier, not worthy to be in the Lord's army of the righteous.

Thinking about it, the memory caused a sudden rush of pain to swell in her chest. She thought she would cry and she didn't want to cry anymore. Not ever. Marvin hit her when she cried. Said she was weak. Thelma didn't want to be weak.

She bit down hard on her lip. She would be strong, worthy of the Lord's blessing.

Marvin's opinion of her made her sad. Hadn't she been a good wife? Hadn't she brought four baby girls into the world? Why did he call her weak?

I've always done what had to be done.

Did he even consider all the time I've spent studying, observing, listening to doctors and nurses talk about infections? All those long meetings dedicated to the one thing they talked about endlessly: preventing infection.

She might not be a real nurse, but she wasn't stupid. The very thing they tried to prevent would bring them down – infection.

Studying, learning about bacteria, buying the necessary materials – a small incubator, a microscope, and several culture Petri dishes – had been an intense ordeal. The streptococcus itself had been easy to get. She simply took a sterile swab and got the culture from her nephew's throat – he was always getting strep. But, she could just have easily taken a swab off of a doorknob, her own nose, or even her skin. Strep was everywhere.

She tried to tell Marvin about her plans, but he wouldn't listen, didn't care. All he talked about was God punishing bad women. He was impatient, wanted immediate results.

When she was ready, everything fell right into place. She'd carefully swabbed some of the bacteria that she'd grown on the blood agar culture, just as the books instructed her, and transported it in special culture tubes that they kept on the Women's Health unit.

The rest was easy. Taneka tried to keep Carrie's abortion hush-hush, but it was impossible to keep secrets in the compact unit. Then Taneka told her to fix the set-up in the procedure room, which gave Thelma plenty of time to pull everything together.

And it really wasn't complicated.

Thelma introduced the organisms into the warmed KY Jelly that was squeezed out on the instrument tray for the procedure.

That's all it took.

When the MD jellied her gloved fingers for a pre-exam, the bacteria was there, ready and waiting.

When she dipped every cervical dilator into the jelly, before introducing it into the cervix, the bacteria was there.

Every time she used the warmed lubricating jelly, the bacteria were there, waiting. All that fresh bacteria was finding a new home in every vessel in that killer's uterus and bloodstream.

And Carrie was only the first. The first because she'd always treated Thelma like a lesser person because she wasn't an RN.

40

I may only be a medical assistant, but I deserve respect. I'm not the unholy one here. You're the ones who sin by helping destroy little babies; you suck out God's gift and throw it away like garbage. You let the real killers walk away to fornicate again and again. Kill again and again.

The law may not make them pay, but God will. And I will help Him.

Chapter 10

Harry Lucke's first day back at Ridgewood was a quiet one. ICU had three stable patients and if everything went as planned, they would end up on a step-down unit later in the day ... or tomorrow.

There was only one other nurse on the floor and Harry had encouraged her to take one of those rare cafeteria breaks ICU nurses get.

With an enthusiastic nod, she headed out and said, "You're a doll, Harry."

Is it sexist to call a man a doll? I'll have to see what Gina has to say about that.

He laughed, poured a cup of coffee, and studied his nurse's notes while he waited for it to cool.

He and Gina had very different nursing goals. She treasured the close relationships that developed with the people under her care, the kind of nursing where she could get to the core of what made people tick.

All of that was secondary to Harry. He loved doing critical care, with its massive doses of high-tech nursing; it not only made him feel needed, it left him with the primary goal of bringing his patients safely through a crisis.

And he didn't like being tied down to one hospital; it was why he'd become a travel nurse in the first place. It allowed him to move from one location to another, check out the different standards of care in different places across the country. It kept him alert and challenged.

But he'd felt he couldn't leave Gina right after the trauma of Nevada. Then her brother showed up, unsettled and troubled. Vinnie really needed all the help both he and Gina could give. And Gina, whom he loved and planned to marry, was scared and distracted now that her ex, Dominick, was out of prison; she was the one who'd put him in the slammer after he'd almost beat her to death. At least the gods were in their favor -- he was in New York, three thousand miles away.

Since they'd come back from Nevada, she'd had almost continuous nightmares. Harry wanted to be with her, next to her, so when she reached out, he could take her in his arms and hold her until she felt safe again.

So, instead of going on the road again, he'd made himself available to Ridgewood on an on-call basis. But they seemed to need him every day in the ICU; he was already a near-regular on the daily schedule. And being the ICU, the prospect of overtime piled on overtime was ever present.

Harry was about to sip his coffee when the ER line buzzed.

"We have a critical female on the way up," said a hurried voice. "Real bad."

Before he could respond, the swinging doors into ICU crashed open. Two ER nurses came barreling into the unit, pushing a gurney. Harry threw on a pair of gloves and helped shove the cart into a patient slot.

The woman was out of it, moaning, shaking, even under the piled, warmed blankets.

"Lay it on me," Harry said. He hooked the patient's oxygen tube into the wall outlet, hung her saline solution with a piggyback of Clindamycin onto the IV unit.

"Patient is two days out from a routine TAB," said one of the nurses. "Absolutely no problems during or post procedure, according to nurses' and doctors' notes in Women's Health."

The other nurse chimed in. "Co-worker said she returned to work, but went through a rapid cascade of symptoms that started with complaints of flu-like symptoms that rapidly degraded to fever, abdominal pain, dizziness, disorientation."

Harry set up the leads for the EKG, respirations, and oximeter readings for the telemetry unit. "She's going to need venting ... she's pretty damn tachy. Look at that heart rhythm."

The B/P unit beeped. Everyone focused on the readings.

"Blood pressure and temp are diving," Harry said. "And zero urine output. Christ, this has to be multiple organ failure."

"That's what our docs said before they transferred her up here," said one of the ER nurses.

Harry's adrenalin raced. "Call the attending," he ordered, pointing at the nearest nurse. "Did they scan her?"

"Yeah!" said the other nurse. "CT was negative for all the usual suspects: retained tissue, obstructions, perforations, foreign bodies."

Back from calling the staff MD, the first nurse said, "Blood cultures are cooking."

"Shit! Her only hope is the antibiotics ... they have to kick in right now," Harry said.

"She was hooked up with antibiotics pretty fast once the doc got the WBC and cultures going."

"Yesterday would have been fast. Let's just hope it's not too late."

One of the ER nurses' grabbed fresh linen, pulled out blood-soaked pads, and shoved a clean sheet under the woman. "Je-esus, she's gushing blood."

All the monitors suddenly went crazy.

"She's flat-lining." Harry grabbed the defib paddles. "Turn it to two hundred. God damn it, girl, hang in there!"

The other RNs slapped pads on the woman's chest as he gelled up the defibrillator and yelled, "Clear!"

Her body arched from the electrical shock, but her rhythm remained flat. He quickly repositioned the paddles. "Turn it up to three hundred ... clear!"

"Again! Clear!"

"Again!"

The attending raced up to the gurney, stopped in his tracks, eyed the monitor and the large puddle of blood splattered on the floor.

"Call it!" he said to Harry.

Chapter 11

Gina and Harry sat on a bench in the staff garden just outside the cafeteria. It was their lunch break, yet neither had carried any food outside to eat. They sat in silence, off in their individual worlds.

Harry was the first to speak. "I feel like I failed that nurse, Carrie."

Gina tucked an arm in his and hugged him close. "You did everything you could for her."

"Then why isn't she here?"

"Harry, we can only do so much for *anyone*. After that, it's up to the gods."

"It really shakes my confidence, not only in medicine, but in me, when we lose a patient. " Harry said. "That's the whole purpose of ICU. We're supposed to save people's lives. It's the only reason we're there." He swiped at a plant near the bench. "If only we'd gotten to her sooner, she might have had a fighting chance."

"Everyone in our department is in total shock. The way Carrie died … it's like she had a back alley abortion." Gina pressed her body against him, kissed him on the cheek, and rested her head on his shoulder. Then she sat up again. "Don't you think it's weird for her to develop septicemia so rapidly?"

"I've been thinking about that myself," Harry said. "Unless it was some kind of exotic bug she picked up."

"We should have a final culture result tomorrow," Gina said. "At least that ought to give us *something*." She laid her head on his shoulder again. "Anyway, they'll probably do a post."

"Oh, yeah, but I *know* she died of sepsis … a classical case."

"I still think it's strange."

"It is.. I mean, she was a young, healthy woman ... unless ... she had intercourse right after the surgery ... that could introduce some nasty bacteria directly into the uterus."

"I didn't know Carrie, but she was a professional. She wouldn't be that stupid."

"Everyone surprises you sooner or later."

"Man, our first day back." Gina said. "What a mess."

"Most people don't have to deal with this, thinking bad things or sudden death happen only to other people." Harry's eyes were very sad. "With us, each day is a reminder that life is short, very short sometimes."

He ran a knuckle across her chin. "What did you think of the department?"

"I think I'll like it. I'm more worried about Vinnie."

"Oh, my little pumpkin, I don't think you have anything to worry about," Harry said, smiling. "Before the shit hit the fan, I called Internal Meds."

"Really? That was so nice of you, Harry. I didn't want to be forced into the big sister role."

"Well, I know the charge nurse there," Harry said.

"Uh huh! One of your exes?"

He leaned over and gave her long, deep kiss. "There's only you, baby."

Gina smiled. "An evasive answer, expertly given ... but acceptable, nonetheless."

"Anyway, she said Vinnie was gentle, kind, and seemed to have a natural ability to work with frightened people, had a way of calming them."

"Wow, that's pretty cool."

"She also said, you'd never know watching him that he hadn't spent years working with people in trouble."

Gina broke out in a grin. "I just didn't know how it would turn out. Vinnie's usually a gruff, in-your-face kind of guy."

"Not today, apparently. Anyway, the charge nurse said that by mid-morning their manager was talking about having to fight off other units that wanted to steal him away."

""Wow! Maybe I misjudged him all these years. But I do know Vinnie has a steel rod for a backbone. After what my ex-husband did to me, Vinnie was out on the streets looking to kill him ... the same night. I think he would still squash Dominick today if he ever got his hands on him."

Harry squeezed her arm. "Maybe his military experience has stripped away that veneer of toughness you always talk about. Maybe now he's more honest about being scared ... about being vulnerable."

Gina's eyes filled with tears. "Harry, I'm so afraid for my kid brother. He seems so done in. That's the only way I can describe it."

"This job could be just what he needs – being with patients who rely on him. It could keep him from stepping off the edge ... keep him from not caring ... keep him from taking his own life."

Gina shuddered at the thought. "We can't let that happen, Harry."

"We won't, doll."

Chapter 12

After work, Vinnie and Helen walked aimlessly, both of them silent, yet strangely wrapped up in each other. Vinnie sensed words would never be important to either of them. What mattered more than anything was the strong current of connection that kept tugging at him. It was something fierce, something powerful that pulled and drew them together. When she slipped her hand into his, he held onto it for dear life.

They ate an early dinner at a little Chinese restaurant down the street from her apartment.

"Do you want to stay at my place?" Helen blurted at some point between the hot and sour soup and the pot stickers.

"We've just met today. Are you sure that's what you really want?"

"Vinnie, I haven't been sure of *anything* for a long time. But I have to go with my gut when I meet someone really special."

"You think I'm special?"

"Oh, yes, Vinnie. You're very special."

He knew Helen would not be a one-night stand, and for the first time the idea of being with only one woman didn't scare him. Strange, it was the only thing that didn't scare him at this point in his life. Maybe it was because she seemed fearless, strong. Even though she was just a slip of a thing – couldn't be much over five feet tall – he felt safe with her. He hadn't felt safe with anyone, other than Gina, for a long time.

"Remember, you can kick me out at any time."

"Oh, I will. Don't you worry about that."

"Maybe we ought to stop at Gina and Harry's so I can pick up some clothes."

She gave him a wide smile.

* * *

"So Vinnie isn't eating with us?" Harry said, wrapping his arms around Gina as she stood at the kitchen sink.

"I don't think so."

"But are you sure?" He buried his head into her black, curly hair, fingertips rode across her hips, slid under her tee shirt. "Hmmm. I really love it when you don't wear a bra."

Gina gave him a wide smile that was lost when their lips met. It was a long moment before she could even remember his question. "It looks as though he came by and took some of his clothes while we were out shopping. He left a note saying he's with Helen."

That caught Harry off guard. "Helen from Oncology? Your buddy?"

"That's the one."

"Man, he's a fast worker. When did they even meet? He just started at Ridgewood today." Harry sat down at the table and watched her dish pasta from a colander onto their plates. He ladled out a rich garlicky sauce, spreading it generously over their spaghetti. "That smells wonderful. Man, when it comes to Italian, no one beats you."

"There're definite advantages to being born into my tribe," she said, laughing. "Making good pasta sauce is sort of embedded in our DNA. It also doesn't hurt to spend a lot of time in the da kitchen witha your mamma."

He reached for a chunk of parmesan. "So how did Vinnie meet Helen?"

"Before work, in the cafeteria. I introduced them. I don't know what it is about that place. It's like a love boat. It can't be the food, so it must be the air. Everyone hooks up there. The two of them had sparks flying within a blink of my introductions. They must have gotten together after work."

"Helen's a good broad."

"Harry Lucke, one of these days I'm going to bite off your nose. It's such an old, disgusting term. I'm not a broad."

"You aren't, but Helen is."

Gina wadded up a napkin and threw it at him.

Harry caught it, laughed, and set it on the table. "Payback for that tickling session you laid on me."

Gina scooted into a chair, placed a basket of garlic bread next to Harry, while he grated parmesan on top of the sauce. She fork-twirled spaghetti onto a spoon and looked seriously at him. "Do you think we eat too much pasta?"

"Is there such a thing?" Harry shoved a huge forkful into his mouth. With bunched up cheeks, he said, "I know this has been a hard day for both of us, hopefully not typical of your coming days working in the new department, but what do you think of Woman's Health?"

"It *was* a rough start. Carrie dying of sepsis. Darn, it doesn't seem fair ... she ... was only twenty-five."

"You'd be surprised how many people die from septicemia."

Gina looked at him. "How often have you had to deal with it?"

"Plenty of times. Those sickies tend to end up in the ICU ... it's a nasty business trying to save their lives. Most of them end up hooked onto ventilators with all their organs shutting down. It's really ugly."

"I guess I've been lucky," Gina said. "I haven't seen a lot of it where I've worked ... certainly not with medical abortions. Everything is sterile ... or at least scrupulously clean."

"Yeah, but it can begin anywhere, even something as simple as a scraped knee can do it ... anyplace bacteria can find its way into the body."

"As you said, nasty business."

"You must have been short-handed with Carrie gone."

"Gone!" Gina said. "God. Harry, that sounds awful ... so final."

"Yeah, I know."

They hadn't finished, but she started to gather up the plates. "Taneka was great. Reserved, but very friendly ... a helluva good nurse. We got Carrie into the ER and she rattled off her history like she'd known her for a thousand years. Carrie got all she needed right away... lab work, IV, meds. ER – all were great."

"And the other personnel in your unit?"

"Well, there're only three now, two RNs and three medical assistants."

Harry said. "What about them?"

"One of the assistants was out ill, but there was Marcia and Thelma. Marcia was really efficient, friendly."

"And Thelma."

"The jury's still out on her. She's a strange one, Harry. There's something ... something screwed up about her."

"Screwed up?"

"I know you'll think I'm nuts," she said, "but it's the way she moves."

Harry's eyebrow inched upward. "The way she moves? That's a first, my little pumpkin."

Gina didn't want to get into anything right now. This had been one of her worst days. Not that she was a stranger to death, in fact there'd been too many people dying around her lately.

Why can't life be more ... manageable?

"Come here, Ms. Mazzio," he said. She set the plates down, looked at Harry. He had that sweet, warm look that made her want to curl up inside his chest. She moved to his side and he pulled her down into his arms. "What is it, doll?"

She was silent, her head on his shoulder, trying hard to swallow her sadness. "Oh, Harry, it's not just one thing. It's everything."

"Tell me."

"I've been so worried about my brother ... so afraid he was going to kill himself."

Harry ran a finger across her chin. "Maybe with a love interest, he'll have something to live for."

"That's not funny."

"Hey, doll, Vinnie's going to be all right. And if he's with Helen, she'll watch over him. You know that."

"She will, I know she will."

"Come on, babe. Tell me, what's the rest of it?"

She was silent.

"Please tell me."

"It's my ex."

"Dominick? Gina, that guy might be out of the slammer, but he's on parole for three more years. He can't leave New York ... and even if he could, he probably couldn't put together enough money to get out here."

"But you don't understand. He hates me."

"I guess I've never understood that. Why? What could you have possibly done to make him hate you? How many times have I asked you that and never got a real answer? Tell me why."

Gina walked to the window, watched some teenagers skateboard down the sidewalk before she turned back to Harry.

"Dominick was a really great ball player ... almost made the Yankees. It was something to watch him play ... and he worked hard at it for a long time."

"You've never told me that. Why didn't he make it? What kept him out?"

"It wasn't me. It was his drinking and gambling. He just lost his way and with it went his stamina and reflexes."

Gina walked to the sofa and collapsed onto it.

"Every time I tried to get him to stop drinking, get him back on track ... well, we'd get into a terrible fight. That's when I turned into his personal punching bag." Before she could stop herself, she was crying ... couldn't stop.

Harry sat down next to her, pulled her close, and whispered, "It's okay, baby. It's okay... you don't have to talk about it—"

"—he blamed me for being kicked off the team ... said he couldn't concentrate with all our fighting." She swiped at the tears, smearing them across her cheeks. "But it was his drinking that brought him down. Not me."

"How did you ever hook up with this guy in the first place?"

"Mostly family pressure ... both families. It was like a dream come true for our parents when we started dating. At the time he was sort of a star on a Triple A team. And there was that golden aura around him. He was so different from most of the men I'd met; after all, he was going to be a Yankee. If you'd seen him then, you would understand. We'd go out and people would ask for his autograph. Everyone fell all over the guy. I guess I was taken in, too." Gina smiled at him. "Besides, all my friends were getting married." She shrugged. "I know it's stupid. But let's face it; it wasn't my best decision."

Harry was silent for a long moment. When he spoke, his voice was harsh. "They should have kept the bum in prison three more years." He kissed the top of her head.

"Let's just forget about it for now, we're letting a good meal go to waste." She gave him a big smile. "You're the best, Harry." She kissed his head, his cheeks, his chin, and finally his lips. "Do you want some desert?"

"Don't light a fire you can't put out, Ms. Mazzio. Right now, feeling you in my arms, holding you close, I have more than food in mind."

Gina looked into his eyes. "Me, too."

Chapter 13

Jody Simms stood under the shower in the gym locker room after cheerleader practice and let the cool water run down her back. She was bone tired and it was getting harder to do all the routines. That worried her.

She was three months late for her period and she still didn't know what to do or who to go to. She thought about going to Planned Parenthood. They were supposed to be really good, but she'd seen the news stories of the one nearest to her home, the one with very nasty people surrounding the place. In the TV news clips, she saw them yelling at all the women going into the building. The thought of it made her shiver.

The water ran through her hair and she thought about how summer had been so much fun. She and the other girls would meet and laugh at everything, at being silly, playing in the pool, talking about clothes, boys.

Her best friend, Sally, interrupted her thoughts by tossing a washrag at her; it landed on her shoulder. "What are you thinking about?"

How could it have all gone so wrong?

"Hey, Jody!"

"Yeah! Hi, Sally. I was just thinking about the movie I saw Friday night."

Sally started giggling. "You're a nut, Jody. Whatever happened to boys? When did they fall to the bottom of the list?"

Jody shrugged.

"I noticed you were a few seconds off in practice tonight."

"I haven't learned all the routines." Jody could feel her face turning red. "I'll get better."

"Come to the house … we'll work on them together."

Jody forced herself to give her friend a wide smile. "Too much homework today. Maybe tomorrow."

"You know, you're packing in too much ice cream, babe." Sally had a disappointed frown on her face. "You need to lose a few. That could be slowing you down."

"You don't think I'm getting fat, do you?"

"Maybe a little." Sally reached out and squeezed her arm. "Are you all right, girl?"

"Yeah, I'm good."

Sally suddenly turned away. "See you later, she said over her shoulder on the way to her locker.

There was something off about Sally, she wasn't herself. She was acting weird. But by the time Jody shut off the water, she was back to her own problem.

She'd heard about private doctors doing abortions, but she didn't have any extra cash. He college fund was in her parents' name and so was her health insurance. If they found out she was pregnant ... well, she just couldn't tell either of them, ever.

The very thought of telling her mother made Jody want to die. All Mom ever talked about was how great it was going to be when Jody followed in her footsteps to Stanford.

They used to be such good friends. Well, maybe not friends, but Jody was able to tell her Mom pretty much everything, and she used to love to hear stories about her school experiences – anything and everything. That all changed when she entered high school. After that, all they talked about were her grades and what she needed to do to get into Stanford.

Jody got it. Becoming a grandmother and grandfather definitely wouldn't fit into her parents' plans right now.

Mom had had to study hard to become a lawyer, then even harder to pass the bar. But instead of working in her father's law office like she'd planned, she'd married and immediately became a wife, mother, and a hostess for her father's parties. And there was a lot of entertaining at the Simms home,

Jody was never going to be *just* a housewife.

She wasn't sure what she wanted to do after high school, but she loved biology and science. One thing she knew — she was going to do something important with her life. Lately, she'd been thinking about becoming a doctor and *really* helping people.

She should have gotten birth control pills when she had the chance. When Sally went to Planned Parenthood, she'd wanted Jody to go along. But Jody said no, she wanted to stay a virgin and not have to worry about things like getting pregnant.

Yeah, sure!

It seemed like only yesterday when she was looking forward to her junior year in high school. Now everything had changed and she didn't know what to do. One thing was certain — she didn't have to be an A student to know it narrowed down to two choices: get rid of it, or keep it.

I'll never keep it. I'd rather be dead.

* * *

Jody was the last one out of the gym. When she walked to her bike, it was already dark and she knew she was already late for dinner. There were no other bikes left in the rack.

She undid the lock and chain and noticed a folded note taped around the handle bars. She looked around, but there was hardly anyone on the campus. She carefully opened the paper. Even in the poor street light she could make out the large, bold letters:

TRAMP

She felt sick. This morning standing in front of the mirror, she'd seen a definite baby bump beginning to show in her belly – not only that, her breasts were always swollen and sore. After what Sally had said, Jody was starting to feel like fingers were squeezing her throat. She broke out in a cold sweat and flashed back to her sixteenth birthday last week.

Her mother, father, and bratty brother had sat around the table laughing and joking when she didn't blow out all the candles on her cake with one breath. They all said she wouldn't get her wish. She already knew that. She'd wished the alien thing growing inside of her was only a bad dream and would disappear.

But it was still there. Feeding off her body, growing so it could ruin her life.

* * *

So stupid!

It had all seemed so sexy and grown up at the time. Summer vacation had started out so great – all those boys around the pool, looking at her, wanting to do it with her. She could see it in their eyes. And the truth? She wanted to do it too. All her friends had had sex. They said it was terrific.

On the Fourth of July, she'd sneaked out to a party and got drunk and had sex for the first time – not only with Richie, her on-again, off-again boyfriend, but also with his best friend, Bobby.

The girls had lied. It hadn't been all that great. It had hurt and it made her feel down about herself. Even though she was drunk, she'd felt more like a piece of meat being tossed back and forth. After the party she refused to do it again, no matter how much they pushed at her.

And then she missed her period. Two periods. When she missed the third, she finally forced herself to take a pregnancy test.

Positive!

When she told Richie she was pregnant, he'd gotten really mad at her. Swore he and Bobby would plaster pictures all over the internet of her messing with both of them.

Pictures? They took pictures?

"You got me drunk."

"But I didn't force you to do it ... and neither did Bobby. You wanted it."

Then he'd shoved her, and she'd shoved back even harder. He'd stood there glaring at her.

"What do you want me to do? Marry you?"

She was bursting with anger, but desperately holding back the tears, not wanting to give him the satisfaction of watching her cry.

The bastard. He just used me. And I let him.

She'd never been so humiliated. She hated to admit it, even to herself, but she *had* thought about getting married, even though she knew how immature that was. She was way too young to get married. Or have a baby.

"No," she'd told him. "I don't want to marry you, but I need help. What am I supposed to do?"

"It's your problem, girl, not mine. You don't even know who the father is." Then he'd smiled at her. No, he didn't smile, he smirked. "You should have stayed a virgin, bitch, not messed with seniors ... 'cause I'm off to college. I'm not getting stuck with you."

"But, Richie, I need help—"

"—and if you tell anyone about Bobby and me, we'll make sure the whole school knows what a little tramp you are."

That seemed like a long time ago. He *must* have told not only *his* friends, but *her* friends, too. Maybe they'd even seen the pictures. Everyone knew about it and they were staying away from her, like she was contagious or something. Maybe that's why Sally said what she said about her getting fat.

Sally knew.

Everyone knew.

Chapter 14

Amory Mason sat at a desk in his basement, buffing his nails on his shirt. He knew it was unnecessary since he'd had them manicured that morning, but he liked to look at them anyway.

Clean, neat, shiny.

He was ready and early, as usual, for the monthly Holy Eye meeting. Thinking of that always brought a chuckle. Hard to be late since they always met at his house.

That's the way Amory liked things – easy, predictable, controllable.

Clean, neat, shiny.

Founder of The Holy Eye organization, a name he gave to attract religious zealots, he described it as a community help group. But his main goal was to stop abortions.

From the start, he could tell that the people he attracted to the cause were rowdy by nature. But like him, they wanted to stop the murder of the unborn.

While he'd always made a big show of camaraderie with his colleagues at the investment firm where he'd once worked, there'd actually never been any one of them that he'd wanted as a personal friend, nor had he kept in touch with any of co-workers since his retirement five years ago at the age of fifty-four.

The investment house had done well by him, yes, but he'd made a clean break. He didn't even have any of their stock in his nicely diversified portfolio.

He'd been fortunate to have the vision and common sense to spot financial opportunities and jump on them no matter how or when they presented themselves. He'd made a lot of money in the stock market and now he was able to do only those things he wanted to do.

What he'd wanted to do most was to put an absolute end to abortion.

The major problem with The Holy Eye, and it was a constant, was that all of his followers thought they were born leaders and should be in charge. He held onto his status by being the first person everyone saw, whether it was at a protest gathering on the streets in front of a clinic, or at the monthly get-together at his house. A few had tried to unseat him, but they were neither smart enough, nor wealthy enough, to out-maneuver Amory Mason.

It also satisfied him that over the past two years since the organization started, the neighbors finally had stopped asking about all the parked cars in their upscale neighborhood once a month. A few had even wanted to join The Holy Eye. Amory was more than welcoming, but he didn't want people who lived next to him being in the group. Sooner or later they would get in his way. He simply told the neighbors that each member was required to contribute $5,000 to be a part of the organization. It was a lie, of course, but effective. All those requests disappeared and so did the parking complaints.

The group had grown to almost fifty members since The Holy Eye's inception. The relatively small number was a disappointment to Amory – he'd hoped it would be two to three times larger by now. Still, these members were the cream of the movement – rabid activists heavily committed to the cause of saving unborn children ... at any cost.

Any cost.

And that alone was what made someone an acceptable member. Those kind of people were hard to find.

His basement rec room was starting to fill up with the faithful. Fifty chairs had been squeezed into the space. And it was rare anyone missed a meeting; within the next ten minutes the room was packed. When he stood, the murmur of voices hushed instantly.

He noticed Marvin and Thelma Karsh were in the front row – they were his most fervent members. Marvin was one of those who attended every protest, walking back and forth, loudly vocalizing their beliefs and goals. He might be a wild card, but he was always ready to engage the murderers who were going into the clinics.

Amory felt lucky to have Marvin Karsh with him, even though his nasty temper was starting to become worrisome. Still, Amory wished all fifty members were as intense.

From the start, he'd had his reservations about the wife, Thelma Karsh, as he did with most of the women in the group. They were too clouded with emotion to make the hard choices. But he had to admit that Thelma seemed as committed to the cause as her husband.

"Good evening, " Amory said. "Tonight, I want to clue everyone in on our updated agenda. This may prove to be difficult for those of you who have day jobs, but it is imperative that we start conducting more demonstrations on weekdays. There simply isn't enough traffic at the various abortion mills on weekends and evenings."

Several hands shot up in the audience, but he waved them off.

"Our stated goal – from the start -- has been to save the unborn. If that means using sick days, vacation time, or just plain unauthorized days off, then that is the way it will have to be done."

He paused just long enough to view the expressions of the audience, and to note there were no poised hands ready to shoot up into the air.

"We are engaged in a battle ... a deadly battle. There can be no time outs."

Amory handed a stack of printed agendas to the nearest person and asked that they be passed around the room. He waited until everyone had a copy before continuing.

"You will note that this week we will again be concentrating our efforts on Planned Parenthood locations, plus a couple of private practice OB/Gyn offices. And I fully expect those of you who have individual anti-abortion projects in the works to keep them active."

Chapter 15

Elyse Kyser sat near the window in the Women's Health Center reception room at Ridgewood Hospital. When she arrived, unlike yesterday at Planned Parenthood, there were no pickets outside of the building with pictures of dead fetuses, or people staring at her with hatred in their eyes; they simply walked along the sidewalk, paying absolutely no attention to her. They were all off somewhere in their own worlds and had no interest in her.

Elyse still wanted to take off, run away, just as she had yesterday. But after that Planned Parenthood fiasco, she'd immediately gotten on her cell phone and Ridgewood was able to get her in for her consultation right away. She'd called at the right moment and was able to fill in for a last minute cancellation.

She was pleased that the appointment for the procedure was for today, her day off. Her boss had warned that there were plenty of others to take her place, others who wanted a job in the fast food restaurant business. *"Any more sick days. Miss Kyser, and you're out the door,"* he'd said, pointing a finger at her.

But today it would all be over and she'd be back to work tomorrow.

This morning, she'd been told, a doctor would place some kind of seaweed inside the opening of her cervix to start the dilation, making it easier to perform the actual abortion later in the afternoon. They called it a laminaria.

"Elyse Kyser?"

Elyse's whole body tensed up. She looked around and saw an older woman dressed in purple scrubs standing in the open doorway, looking across the crowded room, tapping her fingertips on the door jamb.

Oh, my God! So soon?

She squared her shoulders, stood, and walked on shaking legs to the waiting nurse.

"That's me," she said with a confidence she didn't feel.

"Do you have to use the restroom?"

"No." The minute the word escaped her lips, Elyse realized she really did have to go.

"Go anyway," the woman ordered.

Elyse sighed as she went into the bathroom. She kept feeling more and more like an ignorant child.

When she came out, the woman led her past several rooms, stopped at one, and said, "In here!"

Elyse nodded as though she had a choice, and walked into a brightly lit room not much larger than the bathroom she'd just used.

"Undress from the waist down and put your things on the chair." She handed Elyse a drape to cover herself.

Elyse hesitated, expecting the woman to step out of the room. When she saw that wasn't going to happen, she took off her jeans and underwear and placed them neatly on the office chair. The woman's eyes were stern and followed her every move. Elyse held the drape in front of her and when she turned to get on the examining table, she almost tripped over a rolling stool that had *For Staff Only* stenciled in white paint on the black cushion.

She heard an unfriendly "Humph" but there was no attempt to assist her.

Elyse hoisted herself onto the table, opened the drape, spread it across her lap, and sat there staring at the soft green walls. She could smell the lingering aroma of a recent re-paint.

A stand next to the table held a tray filled with the usual instruments that made her detest Gyn exams; the gooey blob of KY jelly had been squirted onto a square of paper, only in a much larger quantity than she'd ever seen before. It made her more nervous. The room was very *medical.* That was the only word that fit the environment. Practical, well organized, and *medical.*

There was a computer monitor lodged in one corner; a wall rack was filled with informational literature on every possible female issue, from menstrual periods to AIDS – all there for the taking.

Tacked above the pamphlets was a large poster in bright colors showing a woman crying. In both English and Spanish, it posed the question: *Is someone you love hurting you?*

No, not anyone I love. Just Thad and his indifference, along with my own stupidity.

Elyse looked up as the medical assistant opened the door to leave. She tried to read her name tag, but couldn't quite see it. "What's your name, please?"

The assistant seemed flustered, then said, "Thelma." She cut off any further conversation by saying, "The nurse and Dr. Forez will be in soon," then hurried out.

* * *

Gina was waiting for Thelma to come out of the room so she could go in and introduce herself to Elyse Kyser. She was scheduled to assist Hannah Forez with the procedure.

She already knew a lot about Elyse. She'd tapped into her computer file and read the history and notes from the nursing assistant and the doctor.

One pill. She missed just one lousy mini pill.

68

Man, that's happened to me plenty of times ... just luck that I wasn't faced with the same problem. At least I wasn't on the mini pill. They don't call them mini for nothing. Those smaller hormone amounts leave very little wiggle room for mistakes. Not taking those ... ever.

Everything else seemed routine – Elyse's health was good, and she had a future contraception plan.

Dr. Forez had listed some of the patient's interests – she was majoring in environmental studies, particularly focusing on ocean health. Gina thought about the aquarium in Monterey where she and Harry went every now and then, spending a whole day wandering around, entranced with the complexities of the sea.

Gina checked her watch. It seemed to be taking Thelma a long time to set up.

She was about to knock on the door when Thelma came flying out as though she was being chased. She ran smack into Gina.

"Hey—" Gina lost her balance and fell hard against the wall, almost slipped to the floor.

Thelma Karsh stopped in her tracks and stood there staring at her. The medical assistant tried to cover the top part of a culture tube that jutted out of her side pocket. "Why were you standing outside the door?" She pointed a finger at Gina and repeated, "Why were you there?"

Gina was stunned. There wasn't a single word of apology coming out of Thelma's mouth, and she had a suspicious frown that seemed to accuse Gina of having done something wrong. It didn't seem to bother Thelma that she'd almost knocked Gina over onto the floor.

"What's the hurry, Thelma? You almost knocked me over."

"You haven't answered *my* question, Ms. Mazzio. Why were you standing right outside the door?" An ugly glare clouded her face.

Why is she so angry?

"And *you* haven't answered mine. What's the big hurry all about?"

Without another word, Thelma whipped around and walked away.

* * *

There was a knock and a tall, dark-haired nurse slipped into the room. "Hey, I'm Gina Mazzio, Ms. Kyser. I'll be the nurse with you this afternoon during your procedure."

Before Elyse could respond, there was another knock and the doctor came in.

"Hi, Elyse," she said, smiling, "I'm Dr. Hannah Forez. Hope I haven't kept you waiting too long." She pulled on her examination gloves as she spoke. "How are you?"

"Mostly, I'm nervous."

"I understand, but we're going to take good care of you. I've already scheduled a counseling session for you right after we're through here. Do you have any questions before we get started?"

A gush of tears rolled down Elyse's cheeks. She covered her face and started sobbing. The doctor pulled off her gloves, placed a finger under her chin, and wrapped an arm around her shoulders.

"Hey! Hey! It's all right. I know there's nothing easy about all of this, but I'm confident you'll get through it in fine shape."

"I'm sorry," Elyse said, barely able to get the words out. "I always thought I was against abortion until *this* happened to *me*." The tears refused to stop.

The doctor snagged a tissue from a box and dabbed at Elyse's face. "A lot of women feel that way until they're actually faced with an unplanned pregnancy." She handed Elyse the box of tissues.

"Look," the doctor said, "we're not here to judge you, so don't be so hard on yourself."

Elyse blew her nose and started to calm down. "I only missed one mini pill!"

"I know how unfair that must seem, but that's all it takes. But by the time you leave here today, you'll have a birth control plan that will fit your lifestyle and you can put the abortion and all that goes with it behind you."

Elyse nodded.

"Today, we plan for your future ... okay?"

She nodded again.

The doctor re-gloved, then she and the nurse positioned her on the table and lifted her legs up into the stirrups. She reached back for the nurse's hand at the head of the table while the doctor sat down on the stool between her raised feet. Elyse could see only the doctor's forehead, but she heard her reassuring words.

"I think you'll find that all of this is a lot less uncomfortable than you might imagine."

"I hope so."

"Good! Now, I'm going to place the laminaria inside your cervix. It's going to soak up your body fluids and expand your cervical canal gently over the next few hours."

Elyse couldn't help but hold her breath, waiting for horrible pain. But there was only a twinge and then almost right away she could feel the instruments being removed.

"That's it," the nurse said. "You can sit up now."

Before she could blink, the doctor was gone and the nurse was helping her down from the table.

Chapter 16

Gina called Harry to coordinate getting together with Vinnie and Helen in the cafeteria for their lunch break, but as soon as Harry answered his cell, she knew that wasn't about to happen – the discordant racket of buzzers, interrupted by the screech of alarms, said all that needed to be said. Poor Harry was obviously up to his neck in crashing patients and probably wouldn't stand a chance of getting away from ICU any time before the end of his shift.

"Make it quick," Harry said.

"I can hear the problem. See you later."

"I may be looking at overtime, doll."

"Got it."

Vinnie and Helen had already snatched a table for four next to the window – her favorite spot. It was like a mini vacation when Gina could sit there and look out at the garden. She waved at the two of them as she got in line for food. She loaded her tray with a bowl of lentil soup, a French roll, some Jell-O, and, of course, the largest cup of coffee available.

"Harry going to make it?" Helen asked

Gina shook her head and set her tray down on the table. "ICU can be a real bitch."

Vinnie wrinkled his nose. "Tell me that's not lentil soup."

Gina looked at his every-thing-on-it hamburger, buried-in-catsup French fries, and smiled. "Go ahead, bro, clog those arteries. Clog, clog, clog. See where it gets you."

"I don't know if I can stand the two of you together," Helen said, flipping the hair out of her eyes and taking another huge bite of her grilled cheese sandwich. "Bicker, bicker, bicker. And both of you pick on such petty things; it's a wonder you even speak to one another at all."

Gina and Vinnie's eyes met, both smiled, then burst out laughing.

"If I was nice to him all the time, he wouldn't think I loved him."

"Yeah, sure," he said before stuffing his mouth with more French fries. The three of them dropped into silence and got down to serious eating.

As the large room became crowded, Gina tapped into the voices all around her. She loved working in the hospital, and she particularly loved Ridgewood. There was always something happening, some bit of new knowledge she could latch onto and use in her own life, or for her patients.

Coming to a hospital, willingly or unwillingly, could be really scary for many people. It was certainly no home away from home. Gina wanted to be there to help those who felt neither hopeful ... nor human.

She sat back, scanned her surroundings. The cafeteria was a great place to observe medical personnel, always an interesting kaleidoscope of color – both skin and clothing. Many, wearing wildly colored and patterned scrub tops, floated by looking like abstract paintings.

She still couldn't decide whether or not it was an affectation for doctors to wear their surgery scrubs and hats here, announcing they lived up to the dictum of *no hair shall fall upon a sterile field.* But it did provide a modicum of individuality in their otherwise structured environment.

Helen piped up, "So how's the Bronx bombshell doing in the world of Women's Health?"

"Ahem," Vinnie said to Helen.

"All right already," Helen said. "I guess now that there are two of you from the Bronx ... well hell's bells ..." She gave an exaggerated shrug. "How's the staff there?"

"I like the charge nurse. Taneka's friendly, professional. She's good."

"Man, I know when I'm hearing a 'but' in your voice," Vinnie said. "That, or you're not really my big sister."

Helen laughed. "I've known your big sister for a while now, too. I'm waiting for the other shoe to drop."

"Yeah, well, there's a medical assistant I don't like."

"What's the matter with her?" Vinnie said, stretching out his legs.

"She's just not right."

Helen looked at her with concern plastered all over her face. "Oh, no! Not again, Gina."

"Oh, don't look at me that way, Helen. I see what I see. And this gal Thelma Karsh is a passive-aggressive weirdo ready to explode." Gina pushed her tray away. "She practically accused me of stalking her."

"Have you talked to Taneka about it?" Helen said. "She might have a handle on her."

"As a matter of fact, I did sort of broach the subject. She thinks Thelma walks on water."

"Man, it must be in our DNA because I know that if Gina says something's wrong, *something's wrong.*" Vinnie reached out, took her hand and squeezed it.

Sometimes I want to hug you to pieces, Vinnie Mazzio.

"Hmmf! I can see I'm outnumbered here," Helen said. "Is there anything else other than 'she's just not right?'"

"Well. It was strange… when I went into the room with the patient — you know, the room Thelma had just set up — I glanced at the instrument tray and she'd squirted out an unusually huge glob of KY jelly for the procedure."

"Come on, sis, what's so screwy about that?"

"Maybe she just likes to squirt the stuff," Helen said, giggling. "Maybe it turns her on."

"It just struck me as strange. That's all." It did sound pretty lame saying it out loud. She glanced at her watch and leaned in closer to Vinnie and Helen – her words began to spill in a rush.

"We had a nurse from our department die from sepsis yesterday."

Helen's mouth formed a perfect O. "Sepsis? Jeez, what do they think caused it?"

"She'd had a TAB the day before. They're doing a post today, but the floating consensus: primary site of origin was the uterus."

"I mean, it's pretty sad, but totally possible with that procedure, or actually a million other things that cause infection. Don't you think?" Helen said.

"After only 48-hours she was dead. I think that's way too fast. Our protocol calls for routine antibiotics post-op so either she had a horrible immune system or something really messed her up."

Vinnie piped up, "Are you sure this is a job you love?"

"It's the people that count, kid."

"Yeah, I know that," Vinnie said. "I really get it. But—"

"Listen, Vinnie. You, me, everyone should be able to squeeze out as much time, as much life, as possible. Isn't that what medicine is about?"

Chapter 17

After the doctor inserted the seaweed, Elyse left the building and then went for a walk. She stopped briefly at a bookstore, bought a couple of magazines, and sat in one of the store's reading chairs and pretended to read. But she was too nervous and returned early to the clinic. She swallowed the medication the nurse had given her and sat quietly in the reception room, waiting for someone to call her in for the abortion.

She was supposed to bring someone to drive her home but she'd kept the pregnancy a secret. There was no one.

She would rather die than tell Thad about her pregnancy, or ask him for any kind of help. He might have been supportive – she at least wanted to give him the benefit of the doubt – but she'd shoved him out of her head. He wouldn't really care what happened to her, she'd only end up being someone he'd knocked-up.

The medication was starting to work; she felt a little better – her situation didn't seem all that important anymore. She dozed off, then was awakened by someone calling her name.

"Elyse Kyser?"

She wanted to cry. It was that brusque woman who had brought her in this morning.

When Elyse walked up to the woman, she saw her name tag and at the same moment, remembered her name.

Thelma Karsh.

The medical assistant looked around the room. "Where is your ride?" Her voice cut through any relaxation Elyse might have gotten from the pills she'd swallowed. The woman rankled her; she sounded angry and unhappy.

"My friend went to do some shopping; she'll be back in an hour," Elyse lied.

Thelma nodded and they seemed to fly down the corridor. Elyse found it hard to keep up, particularly since she was so lightheaded and could only walk with unfamiliar wobbly feet. Thelma took a quick glance back over her shoulder, but kept on walking. She never slowed down and not a single word passed between the two of them.

Elyse blurted, "I thought Gina said she was going to be with me this afternoon." Even with the medication pills and an empty stomach, this woman's stern attitude was making her insides churn. The corridor took a sudden spin. She reached out for the wall and held on to steady herself.

I don't want this woman with me ... I don't want her.

Thelma stopped in her tracks about ten feet ahead, turned, and stood there tapping a foot. "Ms. Mazzio will assist the doctor after I get you ready and set up everything for the procedure." She walked back to Elyse and took her firmly by the elbow. "But we do have to move along now." Thelma gave Elyse a smile that was gone before it could become a reality.

There was something out of whack. Elyse didn't know if it was the woman or herself, but fear curled in her belly and her heart started pounding.

The assistant escorted her into a room, one much larger than the one she'd been in that morning. There were all kinds of equipment around her and when she recognized the emergency red crash cart she'd seen in the movies, a jolt of terror raced down her spine.

"You can undress from the waist down, then have a seat on the table while I get things ready."

Thelma opened a wrapped set of instruments, put on a pair of gloves, and arranged everything neatly. There wasn't really very much on the tray – far less than Elyse had imagined would be needed. But a large glob of jelly seemed to stare back at her just as it had this morning.

She was shaking so hard, she had trouble unfolding her drape. By the time she was seated, Thelma had finished setting up.

A quick knock on the door and then Gina stepped in. She took one look at Elyse and moved to her side, took her hand, and squeezed hard. For a brief moment, Elyse felt saved.

She noticed that Thelma wasn't nice to Gina either. It was obvious that there was no love lost between them.

When the medical assistant left, Gina said, "You seem so frightened."

Elyse started bawling. "I don't know, but I have this bad feeling that won't go away."

Gina wrapped an arm around her shoulder. "Listen, Elyse, we do these procedures every day. We'll take good care of you."

While Elyse tried to quiet herself, she watched Gina check out everything; it was curious, though, why did the nurse stand still for a long moment focused on the glob of jelly?

* * *

Thelma wanted to race out of the room. She felt exposed and vulnerable. She'd carried the strep culture to work and had kept it in a small incubator-like container in her car before transferring part of the specimen to a culture tube in her pocket. She was grateful that the department's policy was to warm the KY jelly so patients wouldn't be jolted by the chill of it. For Thelma's purposes, it couldn't have been better – it allowed the microbes to stay within the acceptable temperature range. She knew her procedure was not perfect and probably had a number of flaws, but it had worked on Carrie to her complete satisfaction.

She smiled to herself.

That's what the books describe as positive clinical testing.

* * *

Starting the IV was routine. Elyse didn't seem to notice Gina jabbing her with a needle. She just stared at the ceiling.

Gina wrapped a B/P cuff around Elyse's arm, took her temp, and placed an oximeter on a finger while the machine automatically clicked as it searched to record her blood pressure. Waiting for it to finish, Gina rechecked the counter and tray to make certain they held everything she'd need to assist Dr. Forez. Then she went to the suction machine at the foot of the table and checked it again.

"I'm not used to drugs," Elyse said. "I really feel wiped out."

"And that's a good thing right now. But you do feel more relaxed, don't you?"

"I'm better now that ... that woman is gone. Why is she so ... so hateful?"

"Are you talking about Thelma?"

"Yes. I know she's judging me for having this done ... for having an abortion. That's how my parents would have reacted if I'd told them."

Gina had to swallow hard not to agree out loud. Thelma did seem judgmental. "Some people are just more difficult to understand than others," she said, smiling at Elyse. "At least I tell myself that. Do you have any more questions? Is there something we didn't cover this morning?"

Elyse said nothing for a few moments while she seemed to study Gina's face. Tears started rolling down her cheeks. "I mean ... I know it was stupid to miss my mini pill ...I know that. But what was *really* stupid was to give myself to someone, allow myself to be so vulnerable … then be discarded like … like some useless piece of trash. That really hurts."

Gina took her hand, squeezed it hard – she knew what Elyse felt. Oh, how she knew. And she couldn't say one word, couldn't tell her how she'd felt the same way with Dominick, how he'd made her feel worthless, too. She couldn't tell Elyse how she'd had to learn, was still learning, to be strong again. That things *would* get better.

"Have you ever felt that way, Gina?"

"I have."

"How do I get through this and start to feel like *me* again?"

"Right now hormones are making you very emotional, but that will subside."

"You mean I'll stop throwing up?"

"Yeah, you will. And as for the rest of it … it's going to take time. Accept that and it'll all get easier."

"But when does that empty, useless feeling go away?"

Gina thought for a moment. "What are you studying in school, Elyse?"

"I'm into environmental sciences, particularly oceans. What we have to do to save them."

"Wow! That doesn't sound useless to me." Gina rested a hand on her shoulder. "That sounds fantastic."

Elyse's eyes lit up. "We need to do something to save the Earth."

"You should be proud of yourself."

The lines in Elyse's face gave way to relaxation.

"Well, when I'm feeling down, I try to remember that who I am, what I am, are things I decide … not some stranger," Gina said.

Elyse smiled and for the first time, she looked young and hopeful.

* * *

Dr. Hannah Forez removed the laminaria, let it drop into a rolling waste bucket while Gina was uncovering the instrument tray.

The doctor adjusted the speculum; Gina focused the overhead light.

"Looks like the seaweed did a great job of getting things started," the doctor said. "How're you doing, Elyse?"

"I'm fine."

"Good, girl!" She said to Gina, "Give the inside a spray of Betadine."

"Now you might feel some discomfort for a second but it shouldn't be too bad." The doctor injected a local anesthetic into the cervix, then picked up the smallest of several dilators and dipped it into the KY jelly on the tray. She looked at Gina, her eyebrow raised. "You have stock in KY?"

"Not me. I'm just broke and middle-class."

"Well, that's sure a lot of goop."

"Thelma did the set-up. I'll talk to her about it."

Forez continued to dip dilators of increasing size into the jelly before using them to enlarge Elyse's cervical opening. When she was finished, she half stood and said to Elyse, "Can you hang in there for another minute or so?"

Elyse nodded. "I think so."

"Good. The suction machine ... well it's a little noisy ... but then we'll be finished. Okay?"

* * *

On discharge, Elyse confessed she had no one to pick her up. Gina arranged for a cab and ended up lending her ten dollars to help cover the fare.

"I promise to pay you back as soon as possible," Elyse said as she sat down in the wheelchair that had been brought in for her.

"I know you will, Elyse. Hey, listen, you call me if you have any questions or need anything."

"Okay." Elyse stuffed her post-op instructions into her purse and looked at Gina a long moment. "Like you said, it was a lot easier than I thought it would be. Thanks for being there for me."

Gina pushed the wheelchair out to the main patient entrance and stopped near the curb.

"You don't need to wait with me," Elyse said.

"Oh, yes, I do. I want to make certain you're tucked into that cab safe and sound."

When the taxi arrived, Gina helped Elyse into the back seat and made sure she was comfortable. They looked at each other for a moment, then reached out and hugged each other.

* * *

Gina was smiling as she walked back to the nurses' station. This was why she became a nurse in the first place. She wanted to be a part of people's lives.

Taneka and Thelma were at the desk, talking.

Gina walked directly up to Thelma. "Why are you dumping so much KY on the surgical tray?

Thelma's face paled; it took her a moment to respond. "I only want to make sure there's enough so the doctor doesn't run out."

"Well, Dr. Forez certainly felt it was overkill ... so to speak."

"Oh, I'm so sorry. I'll be more careful the next time."

Taneka smiled at Thelma as if she were her favorite child.

* * *

Thelma grabbed some alcohol wipes to disinfect the counter at the nurses' station. She sniffed at the irritating fumes and kept an eye on Gina as she walked away, watched her hips sway as if she was something special. She really disliked the new nurse with her heavy New York accent.

Just because she's an RN, the bitch thinks she's smarter than me. Thinks she can treat me like dirt.

We'll see about that.

* * *

Ever since talking to his mother, Dominick had been scouting Ridgewood Hospital, hoping to spot Gina either arriving for or leaving work.

He didn't know her schedule, but assumed she'd work either the day or swing shift. He'd already tried both on separate days without luck, so now he was repeating himself. Today, he timed it to be at the hospital about 3:30, which was about the time she would usually leave work when they lived together in New York. It was close to four and he hadn't spotted her, yet.

He decided that if he didn't see her today, he was going to search the streets around the hospital for her stupid, fucking Fiat. She would never give that up. He tried once to sneak into the Ridgewood garage, but made a quick escape when he saw it was patrolled by a rent-a-cop in an electric golf cart.

Dominick parked his cheapo rental in a *Handicapped Parking* zone across the street from the hospital so he could watch the front entrance. He'd early on realized there was too much ground to cover – and hills to climb – to cover all the hospitals in San Francisco by foot, bus, and streetcar.

There was a lot of traffic today, both vehicles and pedestrians, which made it difficult to keep a close eye on what was happening across the street at Ridgewood. Then, just after 4:00, when he was getting ready to leave, he watched a taxi pull up to the patient entrance. And there she was! His fucking ex-wife was pushing a wheelchair out toward the curb. He watched her help a woman into the backseat of the cab.

"Got you, bitch!"

Two people walking by gave him dirty looks, but he didn't give a rat's ass. What did they know?

"Fuck off," he snapped. "Go home and fry an artichoke or something."

The pair hurried on, didn't look back.

Shoulda told those two boobs that there, across the street, was the skank who not only killed my baseball career, but had me thrown in the slammer to rot for three years.

This time she's not going to get away. This time she's gonna pay.

He watched until the taxi left, moving away from the curb into the flow of traffic, and Gina had gone back inside.

Cold sweat trickled under his arms, a fiery volcano roiled inside. Now he had to find that stupid car of hers.

He knew she liked to park on less-traveled side streets so some jerk wouldn't ding her precious dinky car. He made a u-turn and started exploring all the side streets near the hospital.

Shit! What a piece of junk this is. Costing me a wad of bills. It never ends. She just keeps messing me up.

He was about to turn onto a new street when he saw it.

You don't get away this time, bitch. I'm gonna nail you.

He edged into a space on the opposite side of the street from the Fiat and waited. He'd almost dozed off when he saw her walking down the sidewalk, headed for her car. He waited for her to drive away, then swung around to follow her at a safe distance, hoping she was headed home. She drove into a residential neighborhood, found a spot for the stupid Fiat, and entered an apartment complex.

After she was inside, he double-parked in front of the apartment and walked up to read the tenant names under the individual door-buzzer buttons.

And there it was: *Gina Mazzio / Harry Lucke,*

He slammed a hand against the mailboxes. He'd found her!

Chapter 18

Thelma was on fire – heart thrumming, adrenaline racing through every part of her. She couldn't sit still.

Pace, pace, pace. Back and forth, back and forth.

I actually did it!

A coil of pleasure expanded in her belly. Her studying ... her planning ... her praying had worked.

Oh, when is he coming home?

He had to be somewhere in the building this late in the day. Something must have broken down in one of the apartments or he would have been home by now.

She looked down at their couch and swept a hand like a wand across the sagging seats, as if that motion alone would change the secondhand piece into something brand new, something plush and wonderful. Oh, how she'd wanted to get new furniture, new drapes, new furnishings that would brighten up their living room. But Marvin wouldn't allow it; said what they had was good enough – The Holy Eye needed their money more.

Maybe. But none of them have done what I've done ... I've given one hundred percent.

Since she couldn't sit still, she slipped into her homemade laboratory in the bathroom. She rolled out a small table from the corner behind the door and lifted the cloth that covered a microscope, small incubator, and other equipment. Opening the warming unit she scanned the temperature gauges to make sure everything was optimal for her cultures.

It all looked fine. She smiled when she saw the new growth in the petri dishes reacting to the blood agar. She lifted a tiny sample of bacteria, placed it on a slide, adjusted the lens and checked it under the scope. The strep was ovoid and grew in strings or chains. They were really very beautiful.

She'd known she could do this, but the feelings of accomplishment began to fade when she thought about how much more she'd wanted to know, to understand. Instead of going to college, she'd married Marvin. Then there was one baby after another –all four were girls. Her dreams of college were over. There was never any money left over for Thelma or what she wanted.

She turned back to the microscope.

Thelma had read about Hemolytic Strep but it really didn't mean much, other than it could get into bloodstreams and make people very sick. She knew how inadequate she was with her superficial knowledge. It only gave her very limited understanding about the bacteria she was nurturing.

When she first started, she only wanted women to get really sick. But when Carrie died, Thelma knew she had become the hand of God – through Him she had dished out the ultimate punishment – death.

She was still conflicted about the nurses and doctors? Weren't they accomplices to the women seeking abortion? Weren't they murderers, too?

The new nurse Gina Mazzio popped into her head. Thelma didn't like her – she seemed able to take in everything at once.

Why was she listening to me outside the patient room today? Is she watching me all the time?

She went back out into the living room and plopped down into their tattered La-Z-Boy just as Marvin came through the door.

Looking at him, her enthusiasm cooled. His coveralls, gimme hat, and face were streaked with grease, and his skinny body sagged with exhaustion. She used to think he was handsome, but now he'd lost most of his hair and he walked with a stoop. He looked much older than fifty-five.

He stared back at her with flat, wary eyes, but she knew when she told him what she'd done, all of that would change.

The words spilled from her lips. "I did it!"

Why doesn't he say something?

"I made it happen! Do you understand that?"

She stood and paced around him in tight circles. Before she could speak again, an arm came up and swatted her face.

"Stop doin' that, for Christ's sake," he snapped. "You know it makes me nuts."

Her hand flew to her mouth; it was already swelling and she could feel that her lip was split open. She swallowed hard and held back the tears that threatened to defeat her.

When she swiped at the pain, a smear of blood stained her hand. Rage blinded her and with all her might she pounded his chest. He grabbed one arm, twisted it behind her.

"Ha!" he said, squeezing harder. "You never learn, do you, you bitch!" She was down on her knees now, trying to move, trying to ease the pain. Then she went limp and surrendered. That was the way he liked it.

Far away, up above her, she heard, "Now get up and fix me dinner, ya hear? I've been working on two-twenty-three's broken sink all day."

* * *

Thelma moved very slowly, holding an ice pack to her mouth while she dished steak and potatoes onto Marvin's plate. He was an avid beef eater so she mostly served huge slabs of beef and didn't have to prepare much of anything else. He was a different person when he was eating meat, with a mug of beer nearby.

After a few bites, a rare look of contentment crossed his face.

"Remember that Carrie nurse I told you about?" she ventured.

"Yeah, the one you don't much like."

"That's the one."

Marvin shoveled another chunk of meat into his mouth, followed it with a scoop of creamed potatoes. He could barely get the words out. "What about her?"

Thelma broke out into a smile even though it made her wince with pain. "She's dead."

"Yeah, so what?"

"She had an abortion at our clinic yesterday and died from it." Thelma pressed the ice against her lip harder, hoping to numb it. "And I did it. I made her die... and I set up another one today."

A forkful of food stopped midair as he absorbed the information. Then it fell with a clatter onto his plate. He reached out for her.

"Well, it's about goddam time!" His lips roughly brushed her forehead.

* * *

Marvin stepped out of the shower, grabbed his towel and noticed there was still some grease under his fingernails. He'd stopped trying to scrub it all away; he knew it was never going anywhere.

He stood in front of the wall mirror over the sink and stared at his body – the hair on his chest was mostly gray, matching the stubble on his face. Even though he was lean, the skin under his arms and across his body sagged. He hadn't worked out for years. He could sure as hell see the sad results.

When he finished drying, he dropped the towel and left it on the bathroom floor.

Let her *get it, damn it.*

His mother used to scream at him and slap his face when he did that as a little boy, so every time he left something for Thelma to pick up, it gave him a jolt of pleasure. She was a lot like his dead mother. Didn't like to be pushed around, but a little bit of muscle made her toe the line. Dad taught him that; taught him everything he knew about women ... and Dad had been right ... mostly.

When Marvin got into bed, he saw that Thelma was naked under the covers – that could only mean one thing. He tried to remember how she used to look years ago: soft curves, long black hair around her deep brown eyes, nice breasts. Now, her breasts fell like huge blobs of dough when he touched her.

He thought about Kelly in apartment 223. Today, she'd walked around in a slip the whole time he was lying under her plugged-up kitchen sink. From that angle he could see most everything, including her baby-bump. He remembered how he'd ripped off the silky slip she was wearing. It proved just the right image to get him aroused.

Marvin wrapped his fingers around his cock and turned to his wife. He knew exactly what she wanted ... and he was ready.

Chapter 19

After Thelma fell asleep, Marvin slipped out of bed, got dressed, and left the house. He *had* to tell Amory Mason what Thelma had done. No phone call. He wanted to see the man's face when he told him the news.

* * *

Amory Mason hoisted himself up the stairs, using the banister to pull his body upward step by step. Every day it seemed harder to climb out of the basement, and now, some nitwit was at the front door practically sitting on the doorbell. He couldn't imagine who would be out at this hour of the night, ringing doorbells.

Ding dong! Ding dong! Ding dong!

It really ticked him off. His office was the farthest point from the front door – farthest from anywhere else in the house. But would his wife answer it?

No! Not even if she was home.

And for God's sake it was after midnight. Instead of being home where she belonged, she was still out with her friends, having a good time spending his money.

The ringing bell kept on without interruption as he tried to spur himself up the staircase.

People just don't practice common courtesy anymore. Ring the bell once and wait, for Christ's sake.

If it hadn't been so late, he would have figured it was one of the local snot-nose kids, mouthing into a Smartphone while trying to talk Amory into subscribing to the local newspaper, or some such rot.

As if anyone bought those liberal rags anymore.

91

He flung open the front door, ready to give whoever it was a good piece of his mind.

Marvin Karsh was standing there, almost peeing in his pants with excitement.

"Amory, she did it!" Marvin was laughing like some kind of crazy fool.

"Did it? Did what?"

"My wife is now the instrument of the Lord's justice. A woman has paid the penalty of death for the sin of abortion. And it's about to happen to another one."

The idiot was practically shouting. Amory yanked at Karsh's sleeve until he'd pulled the man inside the house, then slammed the door shut. "What on earth is the matter with you, standing out there and screaming your fool head off?"

Marvin covered his mouth with both hands. It was like he suddenly woke up and was aware of his surroundings. "I'm sorry, sir. I couldn't wait to tell you... didn't want to take a chance talking on the telephone."

"So you come over here and shout it out for the world to hear?" Amory led Marvin into the living room and pointed to a straight-back chair. Marvin sat down, cowed like a dog with its tail between its legs.

"Now what's all this blathering about your wife?"

Amory looked at the man with disdain. His fingernails were black and dirty and he wore a shirt with half his breakfast, lunch, and dinner spattered across the chest.

This time Marvin made a visible effort to calm himself and speak in a normal voice. "My wife, Thelma—"

"—yes, yes, I know who your wife is."

"She works at Ridgewood Hospital. They do abortions there."

"Yes, yes! Go on!"

It looked as though the man was suddenly unsure of himself, out of his depth. "Well, she's been doing some studying on the side."

"Studying?"

"Yes, sir. At first I thought it was nothing but a lot of foolishness. Paying all that hard-earned money for a bunch of books and instruments, even a heat box of some sort. Then when she started using the bathroom to make up this weird stuff … well, I almost threw her out of the house."

"How nice of you. Go on."

Marvin again shifted uncomfortably in the chair. "But she grew some kind of germs on these funny little dishes, and it seems that when the little buggers get inside these women having an abortion." He gave Amory a big smile. "Well, sir, the women die."

"They die?"

"Yes sir! Those murdering women die. And they suffer plenty before it happens."

"Does anybody else know about this, Marvin?"

"No, sir. Just Thelma and me. And now you."

"And you're sure a woman died?"

"Yes, sir. She was one of the nurses that worked in the abortion clinic. Got herself pregnant and had an abortion."

"Well, I'll be damned."

"And Thelma did another one earlier today, but we haven't heard anything about that one yet."

Amory looked closely at Marvin. "Again, you haven't said anything about this to anyone, have you?"

"No, no! Of course not! But I call that justice. Serves 'em right … killing their babies like they do."

Amory walked over to the kitchen and poured out two generous shots of whiskey. He came back to Marvin and handed off one of the glasses.

"Yes, it is justice, Marvin. You and Thelma are good soldiers." He held his glass up and clinked it against Marvin's. "And it certainly does serve them right."

Chapter 20

Oh, my God, I'm blind!

Fear snaked up her throat, other senses fired warnings.

Someone's in the room, circling me.

The furtive steps made her heart flutter until it became wings tearing at her chest – she screamed over and over into a mouth gag.

Fast, hard, loud, furious breathing felt like a windstorm around her.

A man's pacing. Has to be a man. Movements all wrong for a woman. Can smell the sweat ... male, sexual.

Her tongue poked at a wide gash on her inner lip and she remembered. He had punched her over and over until she thought her teeth would crack.

Globs of drool kept dripping down her chin, she wanted to wipe at it, but her hands were behind her, bound with wire that was cutting into her skin.

"Send me to prison, huh" Well, try to get out of this, Ms. Nightingale."

Dominick!

He's here. He's going to kill me.

Kill me!

Gina!

Gina, wake up!

The wire was slicing deeper into her wrists.

O-ooh, the pain.

"Leave me al-o-o-one!"

"Let me go!"

"Gina! Baby, it's okay. It's me, Harry!"

Her eyes snapped open; the street light in the window glowed on Harry's face.

"Harry!" She reached out and wrapped her arms around him, crushing him to her.

"Baby, it's just a dream."

"Dominick!"

"Again?"

"He'd beaten me, tied me up … with wire. He was going to kill me."

Harry squeezed her tighter, his hands moved up and down, soothing her body. She wanted to crawl into his chest and hide.

"You keep having these nightmares ever since we came back to California. What's going on, babe?"

"I know it sounds crazy … but I can feel his presence. Today I was helping a patient into a cab and I could swear I felt his eyes on me from somewhere in the street. He was there! I even looked around for him, but there were too many people. It was too crowded."

"Look at me, Gina." He held her at arms' length. "Dominick is *not* here. Do you really think he'd break parole, risk going back to jail?"

"Don't you understand? He'd do anything to get his hands on me."

* * *

Elyse awoke with a start. A gush of blood running wild from between her legs. When she sat up, the dim light made it look like a huge black stain spreading everywhere.

Oh, my God!

She was afraid to get up, didn't know what to do.

Elyse reached for her cell phone and pressed the auto dial for Jessie, one of the girls she occasionally studied with.

"Yeah." The girl who answered was barely awake.

"Jessie, it's me, Elyse."

"What do you want, Elyse? It's fucking six in the morning and I'm still asleep."

"I need help. Please help me."

"Help you with what?"

"I'm bleeding …bleeding heavily … please!"

"Well, duh! Shove a tampon up your kazoo and leave me alone. I have a test later this morning."

"No, no, no. You don't … Jessie? Jessie?"

The line was dead.

Elyse tried to stand, but her legs wouldn't hold her. She fell back onto the bed, grabbed the phone, and dialed 911.

She passed out before anyone answered.

Chapter 21

Soon, none of the neighbors would be talking to Frannie and Ryan Garrity. She was already being snubbed by the people on either side of them, and she couldn't blame them.

The last couple of nights had been unseasonably warm and they'd had to fling the windows open, even with the rain. Living in a small house in Sausalito, with homes squeezed in all around them, prevented any kind of privacy, especially if you were screaming at each other. They were lucky to have the place. If his uncle hadn't owned the house with several others that Ryan managed, things could have been a lot worse.

When their ten-year-old twins came pounding down the stairs for breakfast, Frannie was so angry at Ryan, red flames of hatred fired her soul. She and Ryan were face to face and they couldn't stop screaming. Without thinking, her hand curled around one of her ceramic sculptures. She was going to hit him. At that moment the girls, still in pajamas, came running into the living room, crying for them to stop.

It was only by pure luck that she didn't hit him, possibly kill him.

"Go back upstairs, girls, I'll make breakfast in a few minutes," Frannie shouted. She let the piece fall from her hand onto the floor, and then collapsed into the sofa.

Ryan's face was a ghostly white as he walked their daughters back up to their room.

"You two get dressed and I'll call you when breakfast is ready."

"Are you and Mommy going to stop fighting?" one of them said.

He forced a smile and said, "Yes."

When he came back, he sat down close to his wife; she started sobbing. "Oh, Ryan ... I'm so sorry. I don't know what happened ... I just..."

"Me, too." He took her into his arms, pulled her close to him; they squeezed together as though some unknown enemy was trying to yank them apart. "Baby, we've *got* to talk about this ... I mean ... *really* talk."

"I know ... I know. But it's so hard to make any sense out of it. You had the vasectomy; it's not like we're irresponsible kids." She tilted away and looked at him – his handsome face was almost as red as his hair, and his soft green eyes were watery pools of sadness. "We did ... you did the right thing."

He slowly shook his head back and forth – a reaction she'd never seen him do. "But we didn't wait the six weeks, Frannie. We stopped using protection a week too early."

"It was only a week..."

"It wasn't enough time."

"I could have the baby," she said, knowing how impossible that was.

"We both knew that having more children was never going to be an option. That's why I had the surgery in the first place. We simply don't have the money."

She knew he wanted to get up and move around, knew it was hard for him to think while sitting still like this. Even when he composed his music, his legs never stopped moving to the constant rhythmic beat somewhere in his head. But he still sat next to her and held her in his arms, probably afraid that if they separated they would start to fight again.

"Frannie, there're only so many hours in the day. I can only teach the piano to so many people ... that's if I can get students at all. You'd think wealthy people would want their children to study music. We barely make it here, even living rent free."

"We could move away, where it's cheaper to live."

"And that's all we would be doing," he said. "Just living."

"I know you're right." She shifted around, saying what had to be said, but already knowing his answer. "Maybe *I* could take on more students."

"Frannie, you're lucky to have the three you have. How many times have you told me how interest in clay work has bottomed out?" He barked a laugh. "Too bad we aren't high tech whizzes. Creative people are just collateral damage now days."

He picked up the sculpture lying at her feet; the light caught the soft abstract swirls. He set it back on the table.

"I thought this was your favorite piece, the one you loved making the most." He ran a hand through her long blond hair and tilted her head up. "No more shouting. Time to think, time to talk about what we're going to do."

"I don't know what to think, Ryan. If we can't come up with a solution on our own, maybe we should find a counselor to talk to."

"You mean, a marriage counselor?"

Frannie saw surprise and disappointment consume his face. "No, no, Ryan, not that." She grabbed his arm, ran her fingers along his jaw. "I was thinking about someone like Planned Parenthood. They must see every kind of situation there is when it comes to having a baby ... or not having a baby."

He pressed her fingers against his face. "That's one of the reasons I love you so much – you're a very smart woman. I'll call right now and set up an appointment ... as soon as possible. Maybe we can even get in today after we take the kids to school.

* * *

Dominick tried to resist the noise. He curled his knees up to his chest and willed himself to drift back into his dream, his favorite dream.

He buried his head under the thin pillow, again tried to empty his mind.

But the ebb and flow of noise, whether it was the loud beating of his heart or the buzz of street traffic, kept invading his favorite baseball fantasy – the one where he made the winning catch that brought the opposing team down.

The ump was waving the batter out. Out! Man, he's out! Double play!

I did it!

It was his time! His time! And now the Yankees were sure to pull him out of their Triple A team and bring him up to the Big Apple. Oh, yeah, they'd been watching him all right. He was having one helluva season. The buzz said that he was in.

Man, I love this.

But the dream kept slipping away. No matter how hard he tried to recapture it, no matter how hard he tried to ignore the racket outside, no matter how hard he fought against it, the noise bored into his brain, getting louder and louder, until his lids snapped open.

Two dudes were in the street cursing each other; fighting over some slut named Beverly.

"You fuck her one more time and you'll be fucking with me."

"Ain't done nuttin', you dickhead."

"Jerks," Dominick muttered.

He closed his eyes again and drifted off.

He floated in and out, in and out.

"Take-a Gina. Take-a the girl out." Ma keeps naggin' at me; Pa gives me that "she's right" look. What do they want from me? Gina, me, we don't even like each other. Besides, I

have a future. A real future in baseball. I'm gonna be with the big leagues. Why bother with some dumb nurse when I can have a really hot chick hangin' on my arm?

The men in the street were at it again.

"Ya hear me? Keep your paws offa her."

"Well, fuck you!"

Dominick sat up. "Always some dumb woman messing up things." Even with the racket outside, the sound of his own voice startled him. And then his stomach did a sudden flip-flop.

Disgusting greasy burgers I've been eating. At least back home, and even in the joint, the food was okay.

He reached out for his watch. Last night he'd plopped it down and almost overturned the rickety bedside table. Now, fumbling with the beat-up timepiece, he tried to focus his blurry eyes. Pain stabbed from the neck up.

"Shit!" He quickly pulled up to a sitting position, pressed his hands to the sides of his head, and squeezed.

He'd gotten into the habit of getting up early, trying to find out what time Gina started to work. And each day he'd felt crappy. He kept telling himself it was jet lag, but he knew drinking at the seedy local bars until closing time wasn't helping. Since he'd left prison with its strict do-this, do-that schedule, he'd been at loose ends. Not that he liked the slammer, but it was what it was, and in there you didn't have to think about what to do next. All he'd had to do was stay out of trouble – with both inmates and ex-mates.

Even now, thinking of the guards and the warden as ex-mates made him grunt with satisfaction. It was a private joke that he never shared with anyone, even the drunks at the bars – he knew it wasn't really very funny, even if he did like it.

He'd hope this morning would be better now that he'd found where the bitch worked and lived.

But it wasn't.

He got up and walked to the window, looked down. It had to be the same two bums still standing in the middle of the sidewalk, foot traffic forced to edge around them while they tossed bullshit at each other. They were saying the same thing, over and over. Dominick watched them sway, fists in the air.

At that moment, he caught the stale smell of beer coming off him. That, along with the stink of his sweaty armpits, gave him an unexpected sense of kinship with the two drunks. He didn't like it.

* * *

Dominick walked down the street and eyed the crowd. He knew he looked okay in his green tee-shirt and jeans, even if everything was new, stiff, and scratchy.

More slant-eyes here in Frisco; nobody talkin' Italian and not one Jew accent. Sure as hell not like the Bronx.

It wasn't just the different mix of people, but for some reason, probably his imagination, everything seemed a little classier, even the panhandlers and the homeless were cleaner, wearing clothes in better condition. There were only a few suits in view, but he guessed this part of town was not where they would want to tuck in to have their two-martini lunches.

The street people, instead of working the lunch-time crowd for small change, or disappearing from sight, many sat out in the open, even in doorways. Store owners came and yelled at them, pretty much saying the same thing: "For crissakes, get the hell out of here! Can't you see you're killing my business?"

Most of the squatters looked up and nodded; it would even look like they were going to leave, but then they'd shift their butts and stay put.

Dominick decided he'd seen and heard enough of these lowlifes for one day. He entered a small café that was squashed between crappy hotels, slid onto a worn leather stool.

The counter waitress kept wiping her nose on her sleeve as she served people their orders. Dominick considered moving to a booth, but that waitress was moving like sludge and her uniform looked like it hadn't been washed in a week or more. Besides, none of the booths was empty.

"What can I get ya?"

"Gimme a burger with some fries ... and I like the spuds soft in the middle."

"Something to drink?"

"A large Coke, with plenty of ice."

The counter was a good vantage point in the hole-in-the-wall café; it wasn't exactly seedy, more like a sit-down-and-run eating spot – Formica table tops, banged-up chairs. The only color in the place was red and white checkered curtains. The café was on the edge of being almost clean.

He was feeling mighty fine, thinking about how he was going to get to Gina, squash her once and for all, when a sudden sense of doom raced down his back and the icy chill of goose bumps climbed up his arms. Like clockwork, these panic attacks hit whenever he thought of about his bitch ex-wife.

She's the reason I didn't make the Yankees; she's the one who ruined my life, put me in the slammer.

Now he was sitting in a puddle of cold sweat.

God damn it! Not now.

But his right arm began to tremble; he tried to force it to be still by holding it down. He felt like he'd been tossed into an ice bath; his skin and extremities were freezing. At the same time, his insides were on fire. His heart felt bunched up like a lava-filled volcano.

"Here ya go." The waitress placed his order in front of him.

His mouth was dry like the desert – he reached for the Coke and drank half of it in one gulp.

This is not prison. I will not be scared. I will eat my food and when I finish I will leave. Not one minute before. But when I walk out of here I will find a way to make Gina pay for tossing me into that slammer. I'll put down that bitch for good.

He pictured her face smashed up and bloody. Her body limp and cold. His heart stopped racing, his hands stop shaking. The vision calmed him. It always did.

Chapter 22

Marvin Karsh was late. Amory looked at his watch again. He needed a ride to the Planned Parenthood site, and he needed it now. He didn't like being late to those protests.

That idiot should have been here five minutes ago. Must have been out of my mind to trust that fool.

He paced on the sidewalk in front of his house, thought about the clinic in the heart of the city. He'd chosen that particular facility for their protest because it was centrally located and had a busy traffic pattern of both pedestrians and automobiles. It was a near-perfect spot to attract the news media, and gain more publicity for his Holy Eye group. Besides, his people needed a place that had a really active clientele, or they'd all be standing around talking to each other.

And, of course he was right. His research also revealed there'd been a news team standing by at the clinic for the past two days.

I need those news freaks waiting and watching for the perfect opportunity to pounce.

Amory focused again on the tardy Marvin Karsh. He stomped up and down the sidewalk, checking his watch every few seconds, disgusted that the fool was now six minutes late.

He pulled out his cell and started to call one of the other Holy Eye members to come pick him up, but before he could punch in the first number, Marvin pulled up in his dirty white pickup truck, the back loaded with placards.

Doesn't he ever wash that thing?

Amory would rather ride in one of the BMWs that belonged to other members, but The Holy Eye attracted more blue collar than white collar people. If he didn't want them to call him an elitist, which he secretly knew he was, Marvin's truck was the answer.

Amory opened the passenger door, brushed the dirt and dust off the seat, and climbed into the truck. As he tugged at the creases of his carefully pressed slacks, he noticed that Marvin was wearing grease-stained jeans and a food-stained tee shirt. Again!

The man never wears a fresh shirt. His clothes probably rot off of him before he ever thinks about changing.

"Didn't you say you were picking me up at eleven o' clock sharp?"

Marvin's mouth turned into a hangdog droop. "Sorry, sir."

The Holy Eye leader nodded and sat with his arms pulled close to his body to avoid getting any dirt on his white, starched, open-necked, Hong Kong-tailored shirt or, his freshly dry-cleaned tan pants.

Still, sitting in this unseemly truck, ready to go out and mingle with his adherents, was like thumbing his nose at every one of the above-it-all financial executives he'd left behind when he'd taken his early retirement.

"What time are we supposed to be there?"

"Just drive, Marvin."

"But the traffic may—"

"Drive!"

Amory looked out the window and sighed.

"Look, Marvin, I want you to control yourself when we march outside the clinic today. You've been getting more and more abusive. We want people to pay attention to The Holy Eye and our message, but we also want to be seen as upstanding citizens trying to protect the unborn. Do you understand?"

"But me and Thelma want those murderers to pay for their crimes," Marvin said, taking his feral eyes off the road for a moment.

Amory finally found something to smile at. "And they will, Marvin. They certainly will."

* * *

Frannie and Ryan Garrity held hands as they approached the large crowd outside the Planned Parenthood clinic.

Protesters walked in a tight circle on the sidewalk, carrying photographs of dead fetuses. Frannie's stomach turned. Tears filled her eyes.

"Let's go home Ryan."

"We can't." He wrapped an arm around her waist and pulled her close to him. "We agreed to do this ... both of us agreed. Let's at least get some counseling. A third party might help us talk it out until we're comfortable with our decision."

Frannie's hormones were out of whack and she burst into tears about everything and anything. At this moment, thinking about running the gauntlet through that screaming crowd started tears running down her cheeks.

She was more reassured and focused, knew what was best when she was with Ryan. But when she was alone, doubts plagued her, poked holes in their logic. She clung to his arm.

The crowd had spilled over onto the walkway in front of the clinic and a security guard was trying to push them back so clients could get to the entrance.

"I know you're right, Ryan." She nodded toward crowd. "But we'll have to walk through all those people. Look at their faces. They frighten me."

"Nothing scary about them, Frannie ... just trying to bully us ... a nasty bunch of fanatics ... all bark ... no bite."

Three clinic-bound women squeezed past the guard to get inside the building as he continued to push back the protesters.

When Frannie and Ryan also edged past the guard, a man broke away and grabbed onto Frannie's arm.

"Murderer!" he screamed. "I hope you rot in hell!"

Ryan grabbed the man by the neck of his tee shirt, pulled until they were face-to-face. "Get your filthy hands off of my wife, you chicken shit piece of trash!"

The man's mouth went slack as though he'd already been punched. Another protester stepped up, pulled him away, and said, "Marvin, this is just what I was talking about."

The words were harsh, but Ryan caught the hint of a smile on the man's face when the news people moved in around them.

* * *

Inside Planned Parenthood, the first thing the Garritys did was fill out a batch of papers dealing with Frannie's medical history and their financial status. When it was time for an exam, Frannie went through the process in a daze.

Afterwards, she and Ryan sat in an office with a Nurse Practitioner, who discussed the process in detail.

Frannie looked closely at the NP. She was kind and it was obvious she had empathy for their situation, but Frannie couldn't control her emotions – she burst into tears.

Ryan squeezed her hand and said, "Is there a co-pay for the procedure?"

"We have a sliding scale for payment, Mr. Garrity. Your part is based on your income. I've gone through your financial statements and it seems a payment of four hundred dollars will cover your share for the procedure.

"I thought this was a free service," Frannie said.

"Not in your case. Your income is too high for that."

"You must be kidding me?" Ryan said. "We're barely getting by."

The NP was obviously distressed. "I know this may seem unfair—"

"Hell!" Ryan said. "My private insurance co-pay is two hundred dollars for an abortion." He grabbed Frannie's hand and they both stood. "I never dreamed Planned Parenthood would be more expensive, or we never would have come here."

The NP also stood. "I'm so sorry, Mr. and Mrs. Garrity, but it's fortunate you have private insurance that will make the procedure less expensive for you."

Neither Frannie nor Ryan said a word. They left.

* * *

Frannie was shouting. "I don't give a damn about what the neighbors think. I'll shout if I want to. I can't believe it. Today was supposed to be the day we set up an appointment. I need to get this over with."

"I know … I know." Ryan looked up at her from his piano seat. His face was neutral, but she knew her husband. He was as agitated as she was. "But even with the large deductible, our health plan will still be cheaper than Planned Parenthood."

"That was a sliding scale? Seems to me their scale only moves in one direction … up." Exhaustion had finally forced Frannie to calm down. She dropped onto the sofa. "We waded through those screaming idiots with their signs and disgusting pictures … all for nothing. You know how they made me feel?"

"They're against abortion and they're trying to impose their beliefs on us ... and the rest of the world."

"Well, you know what *they* can do."

Ryan laughed. "Yeah. I have a pretty good idea."

"I don't need *them* to remind me that this is not something I *want*." Frannie jumped up and paced the room. "What finally decided it for me? I'm sick and tired of listening to spoiled grown-ups complain about their parents not having enough time for them when they were little, because they were working. Working to put food on the table for them." She looked at Ryan. "Is that what our girls are going to say?"

"Come on, baby." Ryan stood and pulled her into his arms. "Let's hope they're smarter than that. After all, they're *our* kids."

Frannie felt better. She'd finally faced the fact they just had to do it. "Where's the nearest clinic that's on our health plan?"

Ryan held up a booklet. "I think the nearest one is at Ridgewood Hospital."

"I'll call tomorrow."

Chapter 23

Gina sat on the edge of her molded plastic chair. She watched the mosaic of doctors, nurses' medical assistants, lab techs press through the cafeteria doorway. Most of them were there to treasure their last moments of freedom before signing onto the AM shift. Like zombies, they headed for the coffee as though it was some kind of life-saving elixir. Waiting to pay, they downed the hot liquid from king-sized cups; they all reacted the same way – that first sip brought a special moment of relief. Gina never tired of watching their expressions. She was sure it mirrored her own actions and reactions.

But on this morning, Gina was nervous. "Maybe they're not coming here before work," she said to Harry. She could feel her insides clutching with anxiety. Had something horrible happened to her brother while he was with Helen?

She had to see him.

"Vinnie did say they would meet us in the cafeteria before work, right?"

Harry turned to Gina, saw her face and took her hand. "They'll be here."

"I'm just worried about Vinnie … I don't want him slipping away from me."

"Hey, doll, look, there they are, and I'd say they certainly have just-got-laid expressions on their faces. I do think *something* is working out for them."

Gina let out a deep sigh; the tension melted. Her gaze followed Helen and Vinnie in the line, looking for their caffeine fix. Watching them hold hands brought back those first incredible moments when she'd met Harry.

It was really strange how the universe could conspire against you one moment, and then in the next, have everything fall nicely into place, like the key piece of a huge jigsaw puzzle.

When Gina first arrived in San Francisco, she'd told people that one day she simply had an urge to leave the Bronx and drive cross-country to the Golden Gate.

But there was a lot more to it than that.

* * *

Even before Gina had fully recovered from critical injuries, the result of a vicious attack by her ex-husband, she knew she could no longer stay in the Bronx, or *any* place in or near New York City.

Her parents kept insisting that she should forgive Dominick and heal their broken marriage rather than testify against him in court.

That was never going to happen.

As soon as Dominick was convicted of first degree felony assault and sent off to prison for three-to-five years, Gina filed for and was granted a divorce. She immediately made plans to leave New York – she could no longer be around her parents or anyone, or anything that remotely reminded her of her ex-husband.

She and her classic Fiat Spyder made the fantastic, awe-inspiring coast-to-coast trek across the U.S., mostly with the top down. She stopped at every tourist and historical spot along the way, taking about twice as long as AAA told her it should take.

She'd only been in San Francisco for a month, and had just finished her second day of orientation at Ridgewood Hospital, when she climbed into the Fiat, lowered the top, turned the key, and heard the infamous click of her temperamental car – its way of saying she wasn't going anywhere on this particular afternoon.

She was exhausted. After an exceedingly stressful day, all she'd been able to think about was going home, taking a hot shower, and collapsing.

She pounded on the dashboard.

The tension of starting a new job, of meeting so many new people whose names she had to remember, had her tightly wound. And then there was the strangeness of a new city – the sounds were different, people talked weirdly, and body language was difficult to interpret. Everything gave off signals she couldn't read. It was all alien to her. So un-New York.

She laid her head down on the steering wheel and let the tears flow.

"Now that's a car you don't see around here very often," said a male voice.

It took a long moment for her to realize someone was talking to her. She looked up. "Yeah," she blurted. That's all she could manage to say after wiping away a mess of tears on a sleeve. This guy was standing on the passenger side of the car, waiting for her to say something else. "You don't see much of this car," she said with a wave of her hand, "anywhere."

Gina didn't want to talk to him, or anyone, but he wore scrubs, so she knew he worked at the hospital; she should be some kind of sociable. And besides, he had the bluest eyes she'd ever seen.

"You're new at Ridgewood, aren't you?" he said.

"And how do you know that?" she said, her hand doing its usual New York flip.

"Well, Gina Mazzio, RN, fresh from the Bronx, who happens to work on the Oncology Unit, I suppose I could give you some kind of pick-up line. But the truth is, I saw you in the cafeteria and asked around about you."

She flashed one of her widest smiles. She couldn't help it – the guy was cute, with longish black curly hair, and, maybe it was her imagination, but there was an aura of special warmth that flowed from those incredible eyes. And there was that smile. It was hard to resist.

He reached a hand into the car. "Harry. Harry Lucke." He firmly, but gently held onto her. hand for a long moment. "And I do believe this really is my lucky day."

* * *

Helen and Vinnie slid into the seats Gina and Harry had saved for them. "Hey, sis, you miss me?"

Helen winked at Gina. "Why didn't you tell me you had this fantastic guy for a brother? I'd have been nicer to you."

"How's the new job going, Vinnie?" Gina smiled at her brother, who looked like a different man. He seemed not only relaxed, but he looked stronger ... more like the old feisty Vinnie.

"Hey, Gina, if you'd ever let on that taking care of people was this great, I might not have joined the Marines."

"Sure, blame it on me, you little brat."

"The word has already gotten around," Harry said to Vinnie. "You've definitely got the touch." He waited a beat. "But how are you *really* doing, kid?"

Vinnie grabbed Harry's hand and squeezed it. "I haven't felt this good in a long time."

"No nightmares so far." Helen reached out and covered Gina's hand. "Don't worry. I'll take good care of him."

Gina felt better. Much better.

* * *

Harry and Gina squeezed into the elevator to go to their individual units. When the door opened for his floor, he said, "Stay out of trouble." He kissed her cheek and was off to Critical Care.

Before she could respond, the door closed. She thought about what he'd just said and fought off the urge to get off the elevator, hunt him down, and set him straight about this staying out of trouble thing.

It's wasn't like she went looking for those gang beatings when she was growing up. Vinnie was luckier – he was a boy. But they'd been raised in a tough neighborhood, and that was that, no changing it. And she didn't marry Dominick because she wanted trouble.

Could she help it if she had a knack for ending up in the wrong place at the wrong time?

No! To all of the above.

Her cell buzzed as she walked down the hallway; she yanked it out of pocket.

"Hi, sis."

"Where are you?"

"Just leaving the cafeteria with Helen. She insisted I call to tell you again that things are really all right. Please don't worry about me."

"Didn't it dawn on you that I might worry when you just moved out like that?"

"Gina, I don't need another mother; I'm old enough to take care of myself. Capisce?"

"Yeah, yeah! To me you're still a dumb kid. Where are you assigned today?"

"Same as before: Internal Meds. Don't you ever listen to me?"

"I'm sorry, kid. I have some things on my mind and I can't help worrying about you. Why don't the three of us take the early lunch slot and play catch-up?"

Gina could hear muffled sounds as he conferred with Helen.

"Okay. See you then."

She hadn't realized she'd been holding her breath until he clicked off. She wondered if Harry thought Vinnie hooking up with Helen was on the list of *troubles* she should *stay out of?*

And what made him say that in the first place?

* * *

Harry knew he'd overstepped the line as soon as he walked away from Gina.

Man, that was stupid.

He thought about the recent business with the death of the nurse from her unit. Right there. That was out of line. That wasn't supposed to happen. He was sorry he'd thrown trouble up in her face, but it was true. She needed to stay out of trouble, even though it followed her like a shadow. No matter what she did or didn't do, trouble always seemed to find her.

He pulled out his cell and hit the button for her number. After getting her voice mail he hung up without leaving a message.

Yeah, she's pissed at me.

Chapter 24

Jody Simms stood in front of her closet-door mirror, dressing and undressing, trying this top with that bottom, adding this sweater atop that blouse. She'd been at it for almost thirty minutes, going through almost her entire closet and dresser of clothes.

If she didn't pick out something soon, she was going to be late for school.

"Nothing's going to hide *it!*" she told her mirror image.

She eventually assembled a jumble of things to wear on top, in layers – a yellow, one-size-too-big tee-shirt over a magenta tank top, both covered by an unbuttoned purple blouse. All three hung out over her oldest faded jeans.

She looked in the mirror one last time. "Only two years to go and you've literally screwed your way out of ever getting into Stanford." She shook her head and sneered at herself before leaving the room to go downstairs.

"No time for breakfast," she announced to her mother as she came rushing down the stairs.

Her mother looked at her, tilted her head to one side, and said, "I thought you gave those clothes away after you lost all that weight."

"Obviously I kept them." She snatched a piece of dry toast off the kitchen table. "It's what I felt like wearing, Mom."

Her mother handed over her lunch bag and kissed her on the cheek. "It doesn't matter, Jody. You always look beautiful."

Jody ran out the door, afraid she would burst into tears. She threw her books in the back seat of her new VW Bug, tossed her bagged lunch on the passenger seat, climbed in, and started bawling. It had taken everything she'd had to act like it was a normal day, that nothing was new or unusual in her life.

Sure. Normal! Absolutely normal. That's me all right.

She knew her mother was watching from the living room window. When she looked up, the curtain was parted and her mom was waving. It made her sad. Her mother was so proud of her, trusted her to be sensible, to always do the right thing.

I've let you down, Mom. Sorry!

Like any good liar, she smiled and waved back.

When she pulled away from the curb, her stomach did a string of flip-flops. What was she going to do?

Something! She had to do *something*! She was three months late for her period.

When she should have been doing homework last night, she'd scrolled through all of the networks and blogs all the kids visited, searching for anything with her name in it. She had to know if Richie or Bobbie had posted something about that night. They hadn't yet, but...

She searched for a long time, but couldn't find a posting anywhere.

In the movies, everyone in trouble headed for Mexico. Maybe she should go, get an abortion down there. No questions. No problems.

Sure, like they're free in Mexico.

The school was up ahead. As she had the past few days, she waited until almost everyone was inside before getting out of her car and making a run for the door.

* * *

Jody slouched in her seat, trying to listen to her English teacher go on and on about a book Jody should have finished reading two days ago. Ms. Wood's voice was soft, so soft that Jody wanted to close her eyes and escape for just a moment.

Not sleeping for the past three nights and worrying the daylight hours away after missing that third period left her exhausted. It got so bad yesterday she'd fallen down during a tricky cheer leading routine and twisted her ankle. Her mom had to come get her and drive her home.

It's not like she didn't try to sleep. She knew she needed to rest, especially after that stupid accident. But she couldn't stop thinking, searching for an answer, hoping for some miracle to save her.

I have to do something about this, something about this thing growing inside of me. It's taking up my space; taking away my life.

Pangs of desperation melted in her chest.

She didn't fit into her regular clothes anymore – only loose fitting shirts like she'd put on this morning were able to hide her growing middle. She couldn't stop poking her belly day and night to see if it had grown.

It had.

Why won't it stop? Die?

Each night, awake in the dark, she tried to be logical, treat it like a difficult math problem – she was very good at math. Jody would examine every segment of an equation, try out every possibility. But X and Y always narrowed down to two choices: keep it, or get rid of it.

Yeah, well, that really left only one possibility: Get rid of it! She didn't want a baby. And even if she did, her mom would totally freak.

Was she being unfair to her mom? Maybe she *would* help.

No. Can't tell her. All she's ever wanted was for me to go to Stanford. That's all she talks about. Besides, she doesn't believe in abortion.

Staring into the darkness last night, Jody had decided there was only one solution to save herself and her family from humiliation.

"Jody! Jody Simms!"

Her eyes snapped open. The teacher was leaning over her, pressing a hand on her arm. Jody sat up tall, looked around. It was only the two of them. The other students had emptied out.

Jody, still half asleep, said, "I'm so sorry, Ms. Wood."

The teacher wasn't angry; her eyes were filled with concern.

"Jody, what's going on with you? You're one of my best students. This is so unlike you. Is there anything wrong?"

Jody felt a gripping chill – she was sure the teacher was looking at her bulging belly.

Oh, my God, can she tell that I'm pregnant?

Jody pulled on both sides of her blouse, buttoned the middle button. "I haven't been sleeping well. I guess it's catching up to me."

"I'm here if you need to talk, Jody."

"No, I'm fine. But thank you for asking." She gave the teacher a silly grin. "Just sleepy."

* * *

A small group of seniors was gathered outside Ms. Wood's classroom. Richie and Bobby among them. As Jody limped by, they suddenly stopped talking and, as a unit, turned and looked at her with salacious expressions.

Richie called out, "Hi, Jody. How's it goin'?"

She nodded at him and kept walking. The group laughed behind her back.

Farther down the hallway, other kids turned to look at her. She felt her face burn. Everyone was staring. They all knew.

Oh, my God!

She almost ran for the door, then outside she saw Sarah, her friend and head cheerleader, talking to the other members of the squad. She pretended she didn't see them and headed for the parking lot. As she opened her car door, she heard Sarah call her name.

Jody waved a hand, climbed in, and rapidly backed out of the parking space, almost hitting someone in the process.

"Watch it!" the kid yelled, giving her the finger at the same time. In the rearview mirror she could see Sarah running toward her. She pressed down on the accelerator and kept going. She needed to get away, take some time to think, and she knew exactly where she would to go.

She was only a couple of blocks down the street when her cell rang. It was from Sarah; she let it go to Messages.

After that, she drove in a daze for a long time until she reached the beach. She was relieved when she saw there were only a couple of cars in the parking lot.

She parked at the far end of the lot, rolled down the windows, and let the ocean breeze cool her flushed face. After a moment, she got out and walked across the sand to where the waters of the incoming tide were lapping at the damp sand.

She took off her shoes and socks, held them in the crook of her arm, and waded out into the shallow waves. The cool ocean water sloshed across her feet.

She tried to remember the Fourth of July party that was now threatening to take away her independence.

Most of it was lost in a drunken haze, with flashes of her lying naked between Richie and Bobbie. The sex had seemed to go on forever ... and it hurt like hell.

She shouted into the wind: "You are a stupid girl!"

She turned and walked back to the dry sand and plopped down.

Chapter 25

Taneka hung up the phone. The black woman's face was a pasty gray; she held tight to the edge of the desk before collapsing into a chair,

"What's the matter?" Gina said, taking her arm.

Taneka said nothing for a long moment.

"Hey, what's going on?" Gina prompted.

"Elyse Kyser is in the ER. She was brought in by the EMTs."

"What happened?"

"Sounds like the same problem as Carrie ... infection. Probably septicemia." Taneka reached for her bottle of water and took several gulps.

"I ... I don't understand," Gina said. "She was perfectly fine when we discharged her. That's awfully quick to go sour ... like septicemia the day after the procedure ... that's *really* sour."

"Two in a row." Taneka emptied her water bottle, tossed it into a recycle bin under the desk. "We've never had this happen before ... at least not since I've been here."

"I saw the post report on Carrie," Gina said. "It's in the computer."

"And?"

"The TAB was complete ... no retained tissue or perforations. No evidence of surgical incompetence. The diagnosis: systemic organ failure, probable cause: Bacterial Sepsis – Streptococcus."

"Nothing to tell us how or why she was loaded with strep." Taneka seemed to be recovering. "Maybe it's just a run of bad luck."

"You really think so?"

"No, but it doesn't matter what I think," Taneka said. "Things are going to heat up around here when Infection Control starts to climb all over us."

Gina turned around and saw Thelma standing near the corridor.

Has she been standing there and listening to us all this time?

* * *

Harry finished listening to the report from the night shift nurse, whose face was as pale as bleached laundry sheets.

And who wouldn't be done in? Twelve hours flying solo because someone called in sick.

"I heard about that post abortion disaster," the nurse said.

"Pretty rough," Harry said. "The poor gal bled out while we stood there ... helpless." He pointed to a computer read-out on the desk. "The autopsy result was just posted. The real deal? She died from septicemia. I'd have bet on it. If I didn't see *that* coming, I might as well give up this gig and start looking for some other way to pay the rent."

"Heard she was one of us, a nurse who worked in the clinics ... Women's Health."

"Yeah, she'd been back at work after a TAB. Gina, my fiancée, works on that floor ... took her from the unit to the ER."

"Septicemia?" The nurse stood, grabbed her purse from a drawer, ready to take off. "Don't see too much of that after a therapeutic abortion."

"True enough." Harry waved the nurse away. "Hey, get out of here and get some rest."

"See you, man."

Harry started moving among the six patients in ICU before the night nurse was out the door. He wondered if he was going to be able to snatch more help – soon as he checked out these people, he was heading straight for the phone – the ratio of patients to nurse was supposed to be four to one. Right now it was six to one, and the day was still young. Guess the bigwigs figured they could get away with slipping in a couple extras.

Like I wouldn't notice?

He knew they'd have a good cover story, but that didn't change the fact that if he couldn't get at least one patient care tech to help him, he was a dead man ... or would certainly feel like one at the end of the shift.

His eyes wandered across the unit. At the moment, none of the alarms were going off and the morning report was fairly benign. It was way too quiet, which could only mean it was probably the calm before the storm.

ICUs were growing, growing in size all across the country. He wondered where they were going to find enough trained people to staff these enlarged facilities. Even Ridgewood's ICU census was supposed to climb to a capacity of twenty when they finish adding the extra private patient rooms currently under construction.

Two of his six were post surgical: one a troublesome laparoscopic gall bladder, the other a bariatric bleed.

I guess we'll be seeing more and more of these stomach procedures with obesity running rampant.

Thankfully, both of the post-surgicals were stable.

Two of the other four were post automotive accidents. He read their telemetry along with the notes he'd jotted down during report. Both were stable, still drugged, and asleep.

He moved to the bedside of a woman who'd had a severe GI bleed. He checked the patency of the unit of blood – half of it was gone and it was running smoothly. This was her second pint, but after reading through her diagnostic radiology and lab work he could see she, too, was stable. If things didn't go south, she might be ready for step-down later in the day.

The last patient was the one he was the most concerned about, mainly because he was a kid. Harry had a soft spot for any kid in trouble. This one had gotten into a whole pile of it.

The fourteen-year-old had taken a small caliber gunshot wound to the thigh. Apparently there was a gang dispute, and even though he was only an outsider passing by, a stray bullet nailed him. At least that's the story the police got out of him.

The lightning bolt tats along the side of his neck told a story of its own. He was a member of some street gang. Regardless, the kid was damned lucky to be alive – the bullet just missed the femoral artery and exited on the other side of the thigh, missing all the major vessels. The exit wound was small and closed and they'd located it quickly by the hole in his jeans.

The kid was sitting up, staring at Harry, eyes fixed and glassy. His crit had been down and he'd just finished a unit of blood an hour ago, but his IV was open and running for whatever else the docs decided he needed.

The phone started buzzing. Harry snatched it up: "Lucke here."

"Hey, Harry. This is Jeff in ER. We're sending up another post TAB. Temp's102 and climbing, bleeding like a stuck pig, and yeah, stat blood work is in and she's being hydrated and hit hard with antibiotics."

"When was the TAB?"

"Yesterday."

* * *

Gina finally reached Harry on his cell again towards the end of the shift. Earlier, he'd told her Elyse was critical, but they were still hoping to save her.

When he answered the phone this time, she knew. "She didn't make it, did she?"

"No, babe, she didn't."

"Oh, my God!"

"Yeah, we were hoping the antibiotics would do something, but whatever bug it was, it really got to her. Nothing we tried even began to work."

"Harry, this is so hard." Gina couldn't stop the tears from rolling down her cheeks. "I told her everything would be all right. I promised her ... and it was a lie."

Chapter 26

Dominick stood in the entryway of a rundown apartment building across from where Gina had parked that dumb Fiat of hers. God, he hated that car. He saw her coming down the street, keys in hand.

He could hardly stand still. What he really wanted to do was grab her, smash her in the face, and choke the life out of her.

This would have to do. He'd have to settle for getting it done and making it look like an accident.

Usually, she had a fast pace because he knew she didn't like walking alone on deserted streets in bad neighborhoods. Today, though, she was walking slowly.

Something's bothering the bitch. Wonder what's going on in that devil's brain.

He got antsy when she got to her car and walked around it. She seemed to be checking the tires before she scooted inside.

He never could understand why she loved that dumb heap. It wasn't sexy or racy like a Corvette. It was just a stupid pile of foreign junk.

Well, after today you won't have to worry about it, Gina, baby ... or anything else. I made damn sure of that.

He watched her unlock the driver's door, look up and down the street.

Dominick took a quick step back from the doorway. Last thing he needed was for her to see him, know that he was in Frisco.

He was ready and waiting to laugh his ass off when the Fiat, as usual, wouldn't start.

It started right away.

Well, that's got to be a fuckin' first. Always came home with more black on her hands and face than a fuckin' grease monkey.

Couldn't help himself – he admired the way she pulled out of the tight parking space without stalling. The bitch really knew how to drive, even if she didn't know how to buy a real car ... a good American-built car.

When she was out of sight, he stepped out and walked up the hill in the direction she'd taken. It took longer than he thought it would.

By the time he reached the crest and looked down, her car was far in the distance – just a red dot parked at the side of the street, at least ten blocks below.

He started really hoofing it, wanting to see Gina crushed and dead in her smashed up car. His muscles cramped and tightened from the exertion. Shin splints hit first, then a stitch jabbed at his side. He wished now that he hadn't turned in the crummy rental.

Man, if I threw a ball now I'd probably fall on my ass. Well, my baseball days are over anyway, so who gives a fuck?

He couldn't help it. *He* did.

In the slammer, all he'd thought about was getting rid of Gina. Now that she would really be gone, out of his life forever, he'd have to think about his future. For sure, breaking parole put New York out of the picture – no way was he going back to prison.

Arizona would be his next stop. That's where he'd go. And it would have to be soon. He barely had enough money left to pay his room rent. Maybe he'd take his small stash and have one big blowout. Hit the bars, find a good poker game -- he might even win a few bucks -- and end up by blowing town.

Fuckin' Frisco costs a fortune to live in anyway.

129

* * *

Gina was sluggish, like she'd worked a double shift. Every muscle ached, and her feet burned. Usually, she walked with a quick step and seldom failed to study her surroundings, a left over habit from living in rundown neighborhoods.

Not today.

Today she was moving with a slow uneven pace; not only that, she'd had to park farther away from the hospital than usual.

When she arrived at the vacant lot where she'd parked the Fiat at the curb, she saw a sign announcing the construction of new housing on the site. It was to start in about three months.

Great! Less parking for everyone.

If she'd been working nights, she never would have parked in this particular spot. Even in daylight the streets in this area were deserted. Gang territory, she'd heard.

Couldn't be any worse than the Bronx thugs I grew up with.

She circled the car. Saw everything was intact, no slashed tires or rips in the vinyl top to accompany the patched pair of tears that were souvenirs from when she lived in New York.

Maybe Californians are more civilized. Three years here and no problems ... yet.

She threw her backpack into the passenger seat and got settled. At least it would be a nice drive back to the apartment at this time of day. She wanted to take the top down, but the threat of rain sat right above her in the form of heavy black clouds that were very low and ominous.

The engine kicked in without its usual sputter or protest. It was tricky getting out of the tight parking spot heading uphill, all while harmoniously controlling the clutch, gears, and accelerator. Too many memories of the car dying.

Today, everything was working the way it should; maybe this would be the best part of a miserable day. She crested the hill and started on the downside.

Gina smiled as the car picked up speed and flew. When it was time to downshift and brake hard for an upcoming stop sign, the Fiat didn't slow.

Frantic, she hit the brake again. Nothing. The pedal crashed to the floorboard and she flew through the intersection, barely missing a car coming at her on the right.

"No!" she yelled.

The hill kept falling away, the brake pedal remained flat on the floor, and the car kept picking up speed.

"Help!" she screamed, stomping the useless pedal.

"Stop! Stop! Stop!" The next intersection, a major boulevard, was coming up fast. She couldn't risk sailing through this stop sign ... someone would be hurt, or killed.

She grabbed the grip of the fly-off emergency brake and pulled back with all her strength. The car lost some of its momentum, but it wasn't going to be enough.

She held her breath, spun the steering wheel hard to the right, and headed for a lineup of large plastic garbage cans.

With a loud whack, she plowed into them. Her visible world turned into a smear of flying debris. Garbage flew up and scattered everywhere. A ghastly roar filled her ears and she was blinded by trash flying into her windshield.

The car stopped with a hard jerk.

Disoriented, dizzy, she heard people all around her yelling, screaming. Someone grabbed her hand, held on tight, but the harder he or she squeezed the faster her head spun. Then her chest started to collapse; she couldn't breathe. It got darker and darker as she dropped through space, plunging into a deep, black pit.

* * *

It seemed to take forever before Dominick got close enough to see Gina's Fiat. When it was a block away, he caught sight of an emergency vehicle coming from one direction and a tow truck coming from another, both arriving at the same time.

The street was a mess. There were vegetable peelings, smashed fruit, and paper trash everywhere; several people were collecting it and shoving it into battered containers. The car didn't look all that damaged. Close up, he saw the front bumper was creamed, and the windshield was cracked, but the rest was intact.

He went up to the tow truck driver. "Hey, man, what happened?"

"Don't know, buddy. I hear this woman lost control and plowed through the garbage cans. She sure as hell made a big friggin' mess."

"So what happened to the woman?"

"Hell, I don't know. I just got here. You'll need to check with the EMTs ... they're loading her in right now."

"Yeah, I see ... I mean was she dead, or something."

"Nah. EMTs reported on the radio that she was okay, but they're takin' her to the ER ... just in case. Besides, they said she's a nurse, so everyone will treat her real good, you know?"

Shit.

Chapter 27

A roller coaster jerked her up, down, slammed her into a steering wheel. Steering wheel? A thunderous roar blasted the air all around her, getting louder ... louder...

G-i-i-i-ina, G-i-i-i-ina. Can you hear me?

Harry?

G-i-i-i-ina, it's me!

Vinnie?

Her eyes fluttered open. Everything was a blur of color until her focus returned. Harry, Vinnie, and Helen were staring down at her, their eyes large with concern.

She tried to sit up. "No," Harry said softly, a hand on each of her shoulders.

"Hey, sis. You had us worried."

Helen held Gina's hand. "How are you feeling?"

"Where am I?"

"You're in the ER at Ridgewood, doll. You were still wearing your ID, so they brought you here after the accident."

"I remember. The brakes went out. The car ... Harry ... it wouldn't stop ... the hill—"

"We've got you now. You're okay, sis." Vinnie gave her a big smile. "Thought I taught you how to stay out of trouble."

Gina gave him a digital salute even though it felt like her fingers were moving in slow motion.

"Stop being such a bad boy," Helen said to Vinnie. "How are you feeling, sweetie?"

"Right now I feel kind of silly." She gave them a smile. "But safe."

"You're lucky to be alive, doll. They want you to stay for a couple of hours, probably in Internal Meds. The ER is hopping, so you can't stay here.

"The seat belt helped," Harry said and squeezed her hand. "But you've got a mess of cuts, and you banged your head pretty hard against the steering wheel. Your scan is fine, though. Just to be sure, you'll need to be observed for the next twenty-four hours."

"I know the procedure, Harry, but can't you check me at home? I don't want to stay here."

"You can be such a pain, Gina Mazzio," Vinnie said, laughing. Helen jabbed him in the ribs.

Gina looked at her brother. "Look who's talking."

"Hey, I can take care of you at home when I finally get away from here," Harry said. "But they snagged me for a few more hours, or until another nurse can make it in. So, why not let the nurses on Internal Meds watch you, unless you want to go home with Helen and Vinnie."

"Please come," Helen said.

"No, I'd rather wait. I really want to go home with Harry." Gina reached out and took Helen's hand in hers. "But thank you."

"How's my little Fiat?" Gina asked Harry She held her breath, hoping for the best.

"You and that car," Vinnie said.

"The car isn't too bad," Harry said. "Considering what *could* have happened."

"Where is it?"

"Don't worry, doll." He leaned over and kissed her on the forehead. "I had them tow it to a garage in our neighborhood. They'll check it out for you."

Gina grabbed onto Harry's arm. "Did I hit anyone? I couldn't see … the garbage—"

"It's all right. No one got hurt. "Harry kissed her on the forehead again. "Pretty smart of you to plow into the garbage. That apartment complex had about fifteen huge containers out front, and from what I hear, one of them fell in front of the Fiat, debris spilled out and jammed under the suspension brought the car to a halt.

"Is that what stopped me?"

"That's what the EMT who brought you in said. Look, now that you're awake I've got to go. I don't want the nurse covering me to start complaining. But I'll see you in a little bit." He bent over and this time gave her a lingering kiss on the lips. He waved goodbye at the door.

"Hey, sis, if you need me. I'm here for you." Vinnie kissed her cheek. "Anywhere ... anytime."

Tears welled in her eyes. "Thanks, Vinnie."

"Me, too. Always," Helen said.

"Hey, you two go on. I'm fine."

* * *

They stashed Gina in one of the empty private rooms in Internal Medicine. After getting settled, she asked the nurses to turn down the lights until she was in gray shadowy darkness.

She closed her eyes and let her mind, her thoughts hang in suspension, floating through the in-between – not really awake, not really asleep.

She had no sense of time or reality; flashes of places she'd been to scrolled through her thoughts like a silent movie.

She knew, or sensed, that someone was close by but her eyes couldn't focus on any one thing. She thought she was dreaming until she heard someone edge around the bed, becoming an undulating ink spot floating around her.

Was it real?

"Who are you?" She heard her voice as a quavering echo.

"Go back to sleep. Everything is fine."

That voice – female – sounded familiar.

"But who are you?"

"No one important. I'm just going to examine your arms. You have some pretty deep cuts here. Why don't I take a culture and bandage them."

That voice belonged to someone Gina knew. Who? She started to slide, began drifting, but then she awoke with a start.

"Who are you?"

"No one important."

"Get out!" Gina half rose to a sitting position. "Get out of here!" she screamed before falling back.

A nurse came running into the room, turned on a bedside light. "Gina, what's the matter?"

"Who was just in here? Someone said they were going to take a culture from one of my cuts."

The nurse flipped on a computer at the foot of the bed. Gina could hear her fingers racing over the keys. "There's no culture order here for you ... why would they? Are you sure someone was in the room? Maybe you were dreaming?"

"That was no dream!"

"Whatever. Anyway, as long as I'm in here, I should tell you that the ER doc thinks we should keep you overnight for observation."

"Oh, great!"

Chapter 28

Jodie hadn't planned to cut school today.

Like yesterday, she'd forced herself out of bed, got dressed, and skipped breakfast, getting a familiar scowl from her mother when she grabbed the lunch bag and took off.

The same routine as every school day, other than not eating any breakfast and having a morning chat with her mother.

She'd planned on going to all of her classes today, told herself over and over that she had to do it. But the second her high school was in sight, her heart started pounding faster and faster until she could barely breathe.

She drove on past the school and again headed for the beach. When she couldn't see the school in her rear view mirror, she was able to breathe again.

How was she going to cope with this mess? How was she going to make it work? All she'd asked for was a little more time to hang onto her secret. Just a little while longer.

Last night that hope was crushed. Forever!

What she feared most, happened: Richie posted some smutty stuff about her on his FaceBook page. Bottom line: she was a whore and slept around – and the post ended with the promise of more to come.

More to come?

She knew what that was. Pictures the guys had taken when she was drunk and out of her mind.

And it wasn't only the pictures. There was plenty more to tell if they hadn't told everybody already. They could let the whole world know that she was knocked up.

Jody tried to keep herself together, but it was as though someone had carved a hole in her heart. At the beach, she collapsed onto the sand, broke into tears.

I am so stupid.

She sat and watched the shallow waves, only a few feet away, come onto and recede from the beach. Everything looked so peaceful, timeless. No school, no pressures, no worries about college, her parents. That's why she usually came to this spot. In the past, right here next to the sea, her problems usually evolved into solutions.

Solutions?

No, that wasn't going to happen. Not this time. She was trapped, backed into a corner.

How could she ever go back to school and face everyone? Even her best friend Sarah was ignoring her, hadn't even called to see why Jody wasn't in class. And she thought about yesterday, in the corridor when all those kids looked at her as if she were trash.

Trash!

They were right. This parasite growing inside of her had turned her into trash. It would destroy her life and there was nothing she could do about it.

Nothing.

Jody thrust her fists into her belly, looked across the vast horizon. The ocean had always been her friend. It had never disappointed her. Today would be no exception.

She slipped out of her shoes and socks and aligned them on the sand next to her. The beach was deserted. It was if she were the only person in the world.

She stood, walked into the water until it was up to her knees – it was very, very cold and she remained motionless while her feet cramped and turned into frozen stumps.

She forced herself to take two more long steps. Her skirt floated on the waves, her teeth chattered; her whole body felt strange and separate.

Tears rolled down her cheeks. She wanted to back away but there was no other place to go. She closed her eyes – she needed to end it, end her fear, her pain.

And she needed to do it now.

Her mind emptied for the first time in three months, and she was calm and unafraid.

She was ready.

Someone grabbed her hand and yanked. A black Labrador barked and jumped at her. She screamed and tried to pull away.

"Hey, what's going on?" An older guy grabbed her around the waist. He tugged, pulled hard until she was stepping backward. "Those waves will pull ya down before ya know it." He smiled kindly but there was fear in his eyes. "Let's go back. Okay?"

Jody was shivering so hard, she couldn't speak. When they were out of the water, she collapsed onto the sand. The man shucked his jacket and covered her.

"Hey, child." He squatted next to her. "What were you doing out there?"

Jody looked at his white hair, weathered skin, and dark brown eyes. "I wanted to sleep in the ocean."

The man was silent as he lifted a thermos. "Brought me some coffee to sit and study the waves rolling in. Want some?"

She watched the steam rise in the cool air as he poured the hot drink into a cup; she reached out for it.

Chapter 29

Harry had talked the afternoon ICU nurse into swapping shifts with him so he could check out Gina's car and pick up a loaner for however long it took to get the Fiat back on the road. He needed to get all of that done before her scheduled release around 11:00 a.m.

On the way home from the hospital, Gina was like a kid just set free from school detention. All she wanted to do was talk, talk, talk. When she couldn't engage Harry in conversation, she began to playfully hit him with a running critique of the six-year-old loner car he'd been given at the garage where the Fiat had been taken.

She also had things to say, at every stop sign, about his driving skills; none of it terribly good.

Finally, Harry reached over and took her hand in his. "Would you prefer to drive with a conked out head, Ms. Mazzio?"

"As a matter of fact, I would. But why should *I* put both of our lives in danger when you're already doing such a great job." She ended the statement with a wide grin and then crossed her eyes. She knew that drove him crazy.

"If you hadn't already beaten yourself up in a fight with a platoon of garbage cans, I'd stop the car and turn you over my knee."

"Uh, huh. You and what army?"

"Oh, my tough little doll," he said, bringing her hand up to his lips, "one of these days you're going to push the wrong button, and then..."

"And then what?"

"You'll just have to wait and see."

She burst out laughing. "I'm looking forward to it."

It was about noon when they found a parking place near their apartment. Harry helped her out of the car, and as they walked to the entrance, his cell buzzed.

"Harry Lucke?" said an unfamiliar voice.

"Yeah, that's me."

"You can get the Fiat some time tomorrow, probably in the late afternoon."

"That's great! You mean it doesn't have to go to a body shop?"

"Naw! You lucked out ... no body damage. Wasn't even a scratch in the paint, which surprised the hell out of me. Anyway, I called around and found a like-new front bumper down on the Peninsula. Should get that later today. And they just dropped off a new windshield. We'll have that installed before the day is over."

"Fantastic!!"

"Yeah, well, I think you should know that this was no accident. Someone cut the brake lines."

Harry was silent for a moment. "You're sure about that."

"Hey, man, you'd have to be flat ass dumb not to figure this one out. A cut line is a cut line."

"What time do you close tomorrow?"

"We're open until six."

"I'll call you tomorrow to set a time to pick up the car."

In their apartment, Gina collapsed on the sofa. "I take it that was the body shop that has my poor little Fiat."

"Nope. It's still at the garage. It didn't need to go to the body shop after all."

"Oh, good. When can I pick it up?

"You, my darling buttercup, are staying home from work tomorrow; you're also definitely not driving." He walked into the kitchen, poured them each a glass of tomato juice, came back, and handed her a glass. "I, on the other hand, will pick up the car after work at the end of my shift and bring it home to you."

"Mr. Lucke, sometimes I love it when you're bossy. But not this time. That's *my* car."

Harry sipped his juice slowly. "Gina, the brake line was deliberately cut."

"So I was right, wasn't I?" She stared at him.

Harry sat down next to her.

Gina set her glass on the coffee table and leaned back into the sofa. "I knew something was wrong. I could just feel it. Dominick! It has to be Dominick."

"Why go there right off the bat?" he said. "As far as we know, your ex is still in New York."

She knew he wanted to snap at her, was trying to remain calm and reason it out. But she knew her Harry, and he was losing the battle. Carrying his empty glass into the kitchen, she could see that he was tense, and the plastered smile on his face didn't hide his true feelings.

"Who else could it be?"

"You were parked in a lousy neighborhood ... it could have been kids ... someone out for a few laughs." He came back and sat down next to her again. "Any number of idiots ... you know that." He reached over and drew her close, held her so tight she could barely breathe. "I'm not going to let anything bad happen to you. Not one thing!"

* * *

Gina was up and out of bed early the next morning, same time as Harry. The bathroom mirror and her aching bones told her she'd really been banged around in the car crash.

They had breakfast together, but Harry was barely moving and looked like he might fall asleep at any minute.

"What happened to you?" Gina asked.

"Kept checking on you," he said. "Couldn't help it. You didn't even wake up when I checked your pupil response with the flashlight."

"Oh, was that you?" She laughed and patted the top of her head. "See, I told you there was no bleeding up here." She pointed to her head. "You are silly. When are you going to give this up? I'm fine. You know they wouldn't have discharged me if I wasn't. In fact, I think I should go to work ... they're short-handed, you know."

"Don't mess around, Gina. We agreed you were taking the day off, and your department's been told that. "That'll give you today and the rest of the weekend to recuperate."

"All right, already. Get out of here, go to work, and come home with my car." At the apartment door, she threw her arms around his neck and whispered in his ear. "Take care, baby. You're all I've got."

He held her face in his hands and looked into her eyes. "I'll see you later, beautiful."

* * *

Harry called her a couple of hours later and filled her in on the autopsy details for Elyse.

Another patient gone. Dead.

When Gina worked in Oncology, death and dying had become a way of life, an everyday occurrence. But in Women's Health?

The same questions kept poking at her over and over – how could Carrie and Elyse Kyser have died from routine TABs? The autopsies said there was no retained tissue in either of them – that would have accounted for the bacterial explosion. But they each had an empty uterus. Nothing there except globs of bacteria that had entered the rest of their bodies, carried by their own vessels. Somehow, deadly bacteria had invaded and started killing both women within hours after their procedures.

Loss of blood was definitely a complicating factor, but it was the microbes that killed them.

How?

There'd been no problem with the procedures; they were as sterile as possible. Everything had gone by the book, routine.

Routine!

Yet, both women were flooded with strep.

A wave of sadness swept over Gina.

Maybe I don't belong in nursing anymore. I've always loved patient care, but lately it all seems so complicated. Is it really the profession, or is it me?

If only she could talk to Harry, that would help. But he'd agreed to start his shift early. ICU was loaded again – eight patients, which might mean his staying on at the end of his shift, at least until they could bring in an extra nurse.

She pictured her guy, with his shaggy hair and bright blue eyes. Thinking about him always made her feel better, lifted her spirits. She couldn't help but smile.

Harry seemed to understand people, but in a different way. He was more down to earth, more real about the loss of life. He cared as much as Gina did, but working in ICU gave him a whole different perspective about dying. It was the kind of outlook she used to have. It was basic, simple – nurses do their absolute best to save lives. That's all anyone can do.

At least, working in ICU, Harry had the latest technology on his side; life-saving equipment was right at his fingertips. That not only helped ground him, it gave him a greater sense of control. Gina only had basic tools and, for the most part, she'd come to rely on her knowledge and intuition to help people. Her gut rarely let her down.

But with Elyse she'd been totally wrong.

* * *

Gina hoped Harry wouldn't call again and find out she hadn't stayed in the apartment as she'd said she would.

As the bus rolled along, she watched the people on the streets, going in and out of stores, sitting at outside tables sipping coffee under awnings and working with laptops, tablets, or smart phones. There were even a few actually reading a book or newspaper. She loved the Muni even though riders were always complaining about it.

Every now and then she felt a little light-headed, but shook it off. She might have enjoyed not having to go to work if she wasn't so worried. But she couldn't let this thing with her sabotaged car slide.

Fortunately, there was a bus stop only a block away from the police station. She walked into the precinct and spoke to the desk sergeant, happy to see it wasn't the same nasty guy who'd tried to hit on her the last time she was here a year ago.

"Would you please let Inspector Mulzini know that Gina Mazzio is here to see him?"

"Is he expecting you, Miss?"

"He is." She smiled, glad he hadn't called her ma'am.

He picked up the phone, spoke softly into the mouth piece. When he hung up, he said, "Have a seat, Miss Mazzio, and make yourself comfortable." He gave her a half-hearted smile. "He'll be with you in a minute or so."

Gina had just sat down on a hard, straight-backed bench when Mulzini came through the swinging gate that separated the front of the station from the back where all the plainclothes officers worked. He gave her a big smile as he walked toward her, one hand extended out in front of him.

"Well, hi, Ms. Mazzio, RN. It's great to see you again."

Gina stood and shook his hand. "Hi, Inspector."

"How about something to eat?"

"I purposely skipped lunch. She patted her belly. "Trying to keep my girlish figure, and losing the battle."

"You look pretty damn good to me" Mulzini said, laughing. "Come on, I'll treat you to a bite."

They walked out the door in the direction of the bus stop. He stopped at a food truck and they got in line. "Tacos or hot dogs?"

Gina burst out laughing.

"Hey, you didn't think we were going for a sit down, did you?"

"Well, I—"

"I'm just a poor cop ... can't take every pretty gal I meet out to eat in this city. I'd need to earn more bread for that." He gave her a big smile. "No pun intended."

"Hey, if you're buying, I'll have a taco with lots of hot sauce."

The Inspector ordered the taco and a couple of hot dogs with "the works" for himself. "I hear you gave Inspector Yee a rough time while I was in Hawaii." They started walking towards a small city park.

"Yeah, well, people expect me to do my job," Gina said. "I expect the same of others."

"You have to give her a little slack ... she has a lot of personal problems," Mulzini said, taking a massive bite of his dog and chewing very slowly.

When they reached the park, a couple was about to vacate a bench; Mulzini and Gina waited for them to pick up after themselves, then took possession of the wood-slatted seat.

"What's going on with you?" Mulzini mumbled through a mouth half-filled with food.

"I need your help, Inspector."

"I'm listening."

Gina took the last bite of her taco, crumpled the paper and her napkin in one hand, and told him about her marriage, from the beginning until the moment Dominick was sent to jail. "Right now, I think my ex-husband is trying to kill me."

"But he's back east, isn't he?"

"I don't know. Maybe he is, maybe he isn't. What I do know is that someone cut the brake line of my Fiat yesterday. My money's on him."

Mulzini took her napkin and paper wrap, wadded then together with his, and threw it all into a nearby trash barrel. "Not much to go on, but I've developed an appreciation for your gut reaction to things. Let me do some checking around, Gina, then I'll get back to you; if not later today, then tomorrow for certain." He took his notebook from an inside jacket pocket and made a couple of notes.

"Give me his name, the prison, and his last-known address," he said.

After she'd given him all the details and he'd written everything down in his notebook, said, "You still at Ridgewood?"

"Yup." She touched his arm. "I really appreciate this, Inspector."

He tipped an imaginary hat. "Anything for a nurse, especially you, Gina."

She knew she was blushing when she turned and walked away.

"Thanks for the lunch, Inspector."

Chapter 30

"I can't do it," Thelma said softly.

"What?" Marvin fired a crazed look her way. Thelma's insides turned to dust.

He's going to hit me.

"I can't do it anymore," she said again, this time in an even quieter voice.

I need to get away, start running before he grabs me.

Her injured leg always slowed her down, never the same after he broke it. She still limped in pain.

His eyes turned crafty. "Say it one more time, woman."

"I have to stop." She took a step back, putting herself out of his range.

He quickly closed the distance between them. "Joining The Holy Eye changed everything, Thelma. There is no *I can't.*"

"Marvin, I almost got caught Friday."

"But you didn't, did you?"

"Not this time."

Without warning, he cuffed her face – her cheek stung. She turned away from him, stepping back again.

"Come back here, you bitch." He grabbed her arm and pulled her against him. "Do you want them to get away with murdering unborn children?"

"It's time to look for another way to make them pay."

"*This* is working."

"I don't want to get caught ... that new nurse is on to me. It feels like she's watching my every move."

"You were supposed to bring me a picture of her. Where is it?"

"I have it in my phone. I just haven't downloaded it yet."

"Maybe it's time we took care of *her*. She's a murderer, too ... she helps with those abortions."

Thelma looked at her husband and again wondered why she ever married him ... and why she stayed with him. She'd known from the beginning that he wasn't all that bright, but he was a hard worker and she'd been at an age where she'd begun to worry that she might never get married. It'd been a bad decision on her part; he treated her like dirt and he'd gotten dumber instead of brighter.

Marvin scowled and latched onto her arm again. "Let's see what Amory has to say about it."

"No!" Thelma tried to pull away. "I don't want to go."

"I'm not asking, I'm telling. You'll do what I say or I'll smash in your ugly face."

* * *

Amory Mason poured 15-year-old Lepanto Brandy de Jerez into a lead-crystal snifter, held it up to the light, and gently swirled the contents around several times before inhaling deeply of the aromatic brandy.

Until a recent trip to Spain, he'd preferred French brandies, such as cognac, Armagnac, and Calvados, of which he considered himself a connoisseur. But it took only one dinner in Jerez de la Frontera to realize it had been a mistake for him to ignore all the gaudy bottles of Spanish brandy on store shelves.

The Brandy de Jerez gave him something new to talk about when dining with friends, whom he suspected had long ago become somewhat bored with his dissertations on French wine and brandy.

He sat back in his Eames chair and let the expensive brandy spin its magic within him.

It certainly wasn't by luck that he was financially better off than the average person. Being cleverer was the key. Maybe he wasn't a member of the one percent crowd, but he certainly was right up there basking in their glow. He relished the fact that he was one of the fortunate few who had enough money to do whatever he wanted to do, when he wanted to do it.

He sometimes wondered if that would have been the case if he'd had a family to take care of. He'd tried; married a lovely girl only a couple of years after graduating from the University of San Francisco. But his wife had had two miscarriages before they'd celebrated their third anniversary.

After waiting another year, they decided to try once more, and agreed that if that didn't work out, they would adopt. She went almost full term this time, then a huge four-wheel-drive SUV t-boned her small hybrid and she was killed instantly, along with the fetus..

It took Amory a long time to recover from the depression that followed. At first he had no desire to marry again, or even go out on an occasional date. But eventually he became quite lonely and started attending church social functions now and then; he met his present wife at a picnic.

The door bell rang; he looked at his watch.

He wanted to slam the glass down on the side table, but resisted the urge and set it down carefully; he didn't want to lose the brandy, or the delicate, crystal-clear glass.

From the comfortable leather chair, he went to the front door and peered through one of the stained-class panes. Marvin and Thelma Karsh were on his porch, staring back at him.

What the hell are they *doing here on a Sunday night?*

He turned the deadbolt and opened the door. Before he could say anything, Marvin Karsh blurted out, "Sorry to bother you this late in the day, sir, but we have a problem. A serious problem."

"We all have problems," Amory snarled. "And how many times have I told all the members of the organization to never come here without calling first?"

"I'm sorry."

"Certainly not as sorry as I am." He scowled at each of them in turn. "If this is some stupid *personal* problem, then turn around right now and go home. I have no time or interest for such nonsense."

"No, sir, this isn't about us," Thelma said. "It has to do with a situation that could be a danger to The Holy Eye."

"And you think it can't wait until tomorrow, apparently."

"No, sir," Marvin said.

"Well, you're here so I suppose you might as well come in."

Marvin yanked at his wife's arm, dragging her inside the house.

"Stop pulling at her like that, Karsh. For heaven's sake, can't you see you're hurting her?"

He could see relief wash over Thelma's face when Marvin let go of her. She gave her husband a hate-filled glare.

Amory walked them into the living room. Thelma's face lit up as she eyed the furnishings. None of The Holy Eye members had ever been in the main part of his home. They always gathered in the basement and never went up the stairs to the living room. Unlike Thelma, Marvin's eyes saw only the bottle of brandy sitting on a chair-side table.

I don't think so, little man; beer or some screw-top rot-gut is more your style.

"So what is so important?"

Marvin, still wearing his grease-stained work pants, started to sit down on a spotless, cream-colored sofa.

"This isn't going to be a social visit, Mr. Karsh," Amory said. "Say what you have to say and then you and Mrs. Karsh can be on your way." He watched Thelma, dressed in nursing

151

scrubs, step between the couch and her husband. She wasn't a pretty woman, but for some reason she'd caught his eye the first time the Karshes had attended a meeting of The Holy Eye.

"Thelma wants to stop doing the work of the Lord."

Amory looked at her. "Thelma, I'm surprised. We've eliminated two women who would have gotten off scot-free without you. Your work has been so wonderful, so valuable."

"Sir—"

"It's Amory," he interrupted. "Please call me Amory."

She smiled shyly at him. "Amory, I'm willing to try something else ... try another method."

"But why?"

Marvin jumped in. "She says one of the nurses has been watching her, and—"

"Have I asked you anything, Marvin? Anything at all?"

"No." Marvin's mouth hung open in surprise.

"Well, then keep your mouth shut until you're spoken to." He nodded at Thelma to continue.

"Well, there's a new nurse in Women's Health, and when I was preparing the KY jelly on Friday, she walked into the room. Almost caught me."

"She didn't actually catch you, did she?"

"No. But I'd just disposed of the extra-contaminated mixture in the trash."

"So she doesn't know anything then, does she?"

"She's been following me, watching me."

Amory sat back in his chair, lifted his snifter of brandy, and took a sip. Marvin's eyes followed his every move. "Let's wait a little longer, Thelma; let it play out for a while and see if she's really suspicious, or if you're worrying over nothing." He set the brandy back on the table, sat up, and looked into her eyes. "Are you willing to do that?"

"Yeah, she'll do it," Marvin said. "I'll see to it that she does as you say."

"Was I talking to you?"

"Well, she's my wife."

"You don't own this woman ... she's not a piece of luggage for you to push around. Understand?"

Marvin clamped his mouth shut.

"So, give it a little longer, Thelma. Okay?"

She smiled at Amory and nodded.

Chapter 31

Harry's right ... Helen has got to be the best thing that's ever happened to Vinnie.

Gina could see remnants of the once-dark circles under Vinnie's eyes as he and Helen walked through the hospital garden. But he was smiling, animated, and there was a definite sparkle in his eyes. Gina hadn't seen him that way in a long time.

And Helen? She was absolutely radiant. It looked like the weekend had been good for everyone

It was difficult coming back to work after three days goofing off, having to explain about her car accident to everyone. But she hadn't said anything about the cut brake line and was now having second thoughts about mentioning it to Vinnie and Helen. Right now they looked so happy, why burden them with this whole Dominick scenario?

But her ex- husband hated Vinnie, too. It wouldn't be right if she didn't at least warn her brother that the creep might be in San Francisco.

The three of them sat on one of the benches outside of the hospital cafeteria – Gina's favorite spot. The sun was out and it was so pleasant. She wished Harry could have come, but once again the ICU was having a busy run and he'd told her he would have to eat lunch on the fly.

Vinnie's gaze settled on Gina. She knew the look.

He's probing, searching, trying to figure out what going on with me.

He knows me too well.

"How're you feeling, sis?"

"I'm okay. I guess I lucked out ... could have been hurt a whole lot more." Listening to her own silly laugh almost made her wince. This was never going to work. Vinnie would see right through her.

Then, as if on cue, "Okay, what's up, big sister? Let it all out before you burst a blood vessel."

Helen looked surprised. "What do you mean? I thought this was going to be a nice laid back, brother-sister-Helen get-together. What are you talking about, Vinnie?" She stared hard, first at one, then the other. "Gina?"

"Yeah, well, seems the Fiat losing all of its brake fluid was no accident. The line was deliberately cut."

"Are you kidding me?" Vinnie plopped his sandwich down next to him. "Who would want to do a shitty thing like that?"

"Harry thinks neighborhood kids might have done it."

"Is that a usual prank for teenagers?" Helen said. "Never mind. I take it back ... who knows what kids will do."

Gina took a deep breath and said, "I think it was Dominick."

Like the aftermath of a bombing, Helen and Vinnie went deadly silent.

Gina watched her brother's face morph from relaxed into violent anger. Red splotches blossomed across his cheeks.

"Of course I don't know that for sure, but in the last few days I've been uneasy ... knowing something was wrong ... feeling something bad was going to happen."

"I will kill that loser if he takes even one step in your direction, Gina. I'll do it with my bare hands if I have to."

Helen wrapped her arm around Vinnie's shoulders, tried to calm him. "I thought the guy was still in prison."

"He's been out for more than a month," Gina said. "But we all know there was never any doubt that he would eventually come for me. It was only a matter of time."

"Yeah, but the guy's such a loser," Vinnie said, "I don't see how he could find two coins to rub against each other, let alone

155

come up with the scratch to come out here. Besides, isn't he on parole?"

"That may not be enough to stop him. Anyway, I got in touch with an investigator friend of mine at the police. He's going to do some nosing around."

"You talking about that cop, Mulzini?" Helen said. "It's been at least a couple of years since I've seen him, but he was terrific."

Vinnie held up a palm. "Mulzini or no Mulzini, I'm moving back in with you and Harry. I'm not taking any chances."

"I can take care of myself, Vinnie. I'm not letting this tear your life apart." Gina bit down hard on her lip. "I shouldn't have told you ... you were both so happy before I dropped this into your laps."

Helen looked at the two of them, frowned, then checked her watch, and stood. "Well that's settled. Vinnie and I are both rooming with you and Harry until we straighten this out—"

"No, Helen, you're not."

"Gina, you of all people know how I am when I make up my mind. Almost as bad as you are. So, we need to think about sleeping arrangements and meals. Let's see, uh, Gina, you'll be responsible for making and serving breakfast in bed on Sundays, unless I'm working, of course...

Gina and Vinnie looked at each other and burst out laughing.

"Hey, bro. It's still not going to happen. I can't handle disrupting your lives. You two stay put. Please!"

* * *

When Gina returned to the clinic, Taneka and Thelma were in the nurse's station having a heated discussion. As Gina got closer, she picked up on the gist of the situation.

"Thelma," Taneka was saying, "you were the med assistant working with both Carrie and Elyse. You're going to come under extreme scrutiny."

"What about you and Gina?" Thelma countered. "You were the RNs present and responsible when the procedure was done. Why pick on me."

"I'm not picking on you, Thelma. I'm merely alerting you. We have two dead patients ... patients that shouldn't have died."

"Well patients die, don't they?" Thelma said, her chin thrust out in defiance.

"Yes, patients die, but not unexpectedly like this. We're talking about two healthy women who died from septicemia within twenty-four hours after surgery. Something's very wrong about that."

Gina watched a sudden transformation from defiance to compliance wash over Thelma's face. Her whole demeanor changed. "Thank you, Taneka. I understand what you're saying. I'd better go now and get the room ready for the next TAB."

"You're right," Taneka said. "Go ahead."

Thelma barely acknowledged Gina's presence. She turned and left the station.

"Why is Thelma so angry?"

"That's a good question. It's so unlike her."

Gina kept her feelings about Thelma to herself, but she did want to hurry along and see how Thelma was dealing with readying the procedure room. Taneka touched her sleeve, indicated she wanted to talk to her.

"Infection Control is going to be all over us, Gina, checking our protocols, procedures, and our techniques ... anything that has to do with TABs. They'll check and double check everything we do from now on. I'm going to need your help getting us through this, okay?" She turned to a pile of forms in front of her. "And that's on top of the usual pile of stuff that needs to get done each day."

"Yeah, I'll do what I can. Right now, I'd better get moving, make sure everything is properly set up for this afternoon's procedure."

Gina headed for the room where Thelma had gone to set up. Outside the door, she stood listening, heard nothing. She took a deep breath and flung open the door.

Thelma looked up at Gina, obviously startled by the sudden intrusion; she was holding a cotton applicator over a dab of KY Jelly on the tray.

"What are you doing, Thelma?"

The woman's face lost its color; she started to say something, but couldn't seem to get any words to come out.

Gina stepped into the room and closed the door. "I said, what are you doing?"

"I was just getting rid of the extra jelly ... I know how upset you got with me last time." She threw the applicator into the trash. "I don't know why I have such a heavy hand squeezing out that stuff."

"I don't either."

"Well, everything's set up now."

Gina could see that Thelma was intimidated. That in itself was surprising –the medical assistant was usually antagonistic around her, never at a loss for words. She watched Thelma as she quickly and silently slipped past her and left the room.

Gina went to the trash and saw the applicator there, covered with an excessive amount of KY jelly. Then she remembered something.

She was carrying a culture tube in her pocket again. Why?

Chapter 32

Jody Simms dashed past her mother, flew up the steps two at a time, and sprinted down the hall to her room. She slammed the door, locked it, and threw her back pack into a corner.

She'd gone back to school today, trying to feel normal again, but it had been the worst day of her life.

She took a couple of deep breathes to quiet herself, but it didn't help. Rushing to her desk, she slid into the seat, and booted up the computer. Her hands trembled as she brought up Richie's website, hoping against hope that he hadn't posted pictures of her. That it was all just whispered school gossip.

Would he deliberately hurt me like that?

But there it was. Just like she'd overheard in the hallway between the second and third periods.

A posted video opened with a close-up of Jody's drunken, mascara-smeared face, laughing and singing. The camera zoomed in on her naked body and followed her as she jumped on a bed, fell to her back, and spread her legs.

She watched in horror as her on-screen image called out, "Richie come to Jody. Jody wants to eat you up."

Jody covered her mouth, smothered her screams during the rest of the clip. She wished that man had never pulled her out of the water. That she'd drowned.

This was so humiliating. So bad, bad, bad!

What hurt most was that at the time she'd thought Richie had really cared about her. Now she saw the terrible truth: he'd played her so he could get into her pants.

Just a filthy little game for him and his friends.

That's all any of it had meant.

She moaned, bent into herself and rocked over and over – pain lashed through her belly, through her chest; it wouldn't stop.

"Jody! What's going on in there?" Why are you home so early?"

Her mother was standing outside her door.

"Jody! Answer me! Open the door!"

"Go away, Mom! Leave me alone!"

"Sweetie, whatever's wrong ... whatever it is, please talk to me. We can fix it. Just talk to me."

Tears flooded Jody's face. "You can't fix this, mom," she murmured. "Nobody can."

"I'm right here, sweetie. I wish you'd talk to me."

Jody's stomach clenched into a ball; she ran to her bathroom, retched until her throat was raw, on fire.

She clamped a wet washrag against her mouth, stumbled back into the bedroom, stood in front of the full-length mirror and turned sideways. Her belly was growing almost before her eyes.

She made up her mind. There was no other way. And with that decision came a sense of peace. She would finally have some control over her life.

She tore off her skirt and panties and threw them into a corner, then flung open the doors to her walk-in closet. The TV special on teenage pregnancies streamed through her mind. The documentary had told her what she needed. But all she could see in the closet were plastic hangers. She shoved and pulled at her hanging clothes. Then, at the back end of the rack, she found what she was looking for – a few empty wire hangers from the dry cleaners.

Her heart raced, her breathing was rapid. The small room started to spin; she grabbed for the door jamb, steadied herself, and took a couple of deep breaths.

She pulled one of the hangers from the rod inched her way along the wall until she was back in the bathroom. She washed the hanger with soap and hot water, straightened the wire, and twisted one end into a small hook.

"Have to. Have to!"

The sound of her voice soothed her as she sat on the edge of toilet seat, legs spread wide. Eyes closed, she slowly inched the wire inside her vagina. She tried to be careful, gentle, but almost immediately the hook tapped against her cervix, a barrier she couldn't get through.

With a deep breath, she counted to five and plunged the wire inside as far as she could, and then twirled it around and around.

Spasms of pain exploded into blinding red and orange bursts; her screams filled her world. She fell to the floor and a gush of fluid raced down her legs.

"It has to be gone! Gone! Gone! *Gone!*" She screamed against the pain as she continued to twirl the wire hanger.

"Jody?"

From somewhere far away, her mother was screeching her name again and again.

Everything was spinning; the light was fading, fading, gone.

* * *

Jody heard a buzz and a muffled noise of something moving around her. She opened her eyes; she was in the back of a truck filled with medical equipment.

"Where am I?"

"Hi, Jody, I'm John, an EMT" said a male voice. "We came to your house to help. We're on the way to the hospital."

"Tell me."

"What?"

"Did I get rid of that ... that ... thing?"

The EMT said nothing.

Everything was roiling inside. She screamed at the top of her lungs. "Tell me! Tell me it's gone!"

Someone else took her hand. She turned her head and saw her mother on the other side.

"You could have told me, Jodie, told me anything." Her mother's face looked strange and old. "I could have helped you ... you didn't have to do this."

Jody turned back to the EMT, who was adjusting an IV line that disappeared somewhere into her arm, someplace she couldn't see. His eyes were kind, concerned, and without saying it, they told her she was in bad trouble.

"How's the pain, kid?"

"It hurts really bad. She grabbed his jacket. "I'm ... I'm so scared."

"Let me give you more morphine. It'll help."

Jodie nodded, then turned to her mom, who was sobbing. "I'm sorry, mom, I didn't want to disappoint you. It just happened ... please forgive me."

Her mother kissed her hand, said something, but Jody was growing so dizzy and she was falling, falling...

Down into nothingness.

* * *

Harry scanned through Jody's history: sixteen years old, twelve plus weeks pregnant, tried to self abort. Post surgery: Hysterectomy and bowel repair.

With a wire hanger, for God's sake. Tore up everything. Why the hell didn't she go to Planned Parenthood? This is nuts!

He read further into the report. The mother had spoken to the patient's best friend, who admitted to having witnessed cyber bullying of the patient without reporting it.

Fucking kids.

Jody was holding her own at the moment. She'd lost a lot of blood and they'd been pushing it and antibiotics from the moment she'd entered Ridgewood around noon.

Surgery, blood, fluids, and antibiotics would have to do the job of saving her life. It was all they had.

Jeez, sixteen years old.

He looked across the room at the mother sitting next to the bed. She looked exhausted; he'd heard the father was out of town. Harry had a pretty good idea of what that mom was going through. He'd seen a lot of mothers lose their children. Not for this, but what's the difference? When you love someone and they're taken away from you, does it really matter what caused it?

Damn right it does!

Kid didn't have cancer, have some genetic dysfunction, wasn't in an automobile accident. She didn't have to go through all of this misery. She could have simply had a safe abortion.

And what the hell is going on with kids abusing each other on the internet? That's pretty fucking sick.

He hadn't heard Jody's mother approach the nurses' station. It caught him off guard when she spoke.

"Would you please keep an eye on Jody? I have to try to reach my husband again." Her voice was barely audible.

"Of course," Harry said. He smiled at the woman. "That's what we do, Mrs. Simms."

Harry knew the mother was watching him as he walked to Jody's bed. Apparently satisfied, she left the unit. He checked the telemetry —the girl's heart beat was flying, even with additional oxygen, her breathing was rapid, and her temp was climbing dramatically. When he gently touched her belly, the flesh became a tight spasm.

"Mom!" she screamed.

Damn it! She's gone sour in just five fucking minutes!

Harry called out to the other nurse, "Tara, get the attending ... now!"

Jody opened her eyes. "Help me. Please help me." She reached out for Harry's hand and clutched it tightly. She looked so young, so small, so sick.

Her B/P was crashing and her breathing was so rapid now she couldn't speak anymore, even though she tried. Her mouth kept opening and closing but her voice was swallowed. Tara moved to the other side of the bed. "Jesus, Harry, she's in shock."

"Damn it, her heart's stopped." Harry said. "Start CPR while I get the defib going."

Tara started pressing down rhythmically on Jody's chest while Harry readied the paddles. "Clear!"

Tara held her hands up in the air.

The shock made Jody's body arch, but it did nothing to start her heart beating again.

"Clear." Harry called out again. Jody's body arched again, but there was still no response.

The attending hurried in, called out, "Hit it again!"

The three of them stared at the telemetry after the jolt.

Nothing.

Harry knew the MD was going to call it.

'Let's try one more time," Harry said.

"Okay. Go!"

"Clear," Harry said, paddles placed and ready on her chest.

He held his breath, watched the flat line, hoping for a blip that would give him some hope.

But Jody was gone.

"Call it," the attending said.

At that moment, the girl's mother walked back into the ICU. She ran to the bed and started screaming, "No! No! No!" She grabbed her daughter's limp arm. "Jody! No, please, no!"

"Time: 2:58 p.m.

Chapter 33

"We lost a sixteen-year-old girl a little while ago."

Gina held the phone tight against her ear. "Oh, Harry, another death? What a horrible way for you to start the week."

"Yeah, you can certainly say that."

"What did she die of?"

"Tried to get rid of a three-month pregnancy with a coat hanger. Tore up her whole insides – ripped her cervix, uterus, and punctured her bowel. She might as well have swallowed cyanide. It would have killed her quicker ... and with a lot less pain."

"I don't understand. Why didn't the poor kid go for a legal abortion?"

"Kids! Who knows what her thinking was, other than she was probably scared out of her mind."

"I'm so sorry, Harry. That must have been really, really hard for you."

"Listen, babe, I'm going to hang out with the mother for a while. She's totally destroyed and the husband is out of town. We had to sedate the poor woman ... she's in no condition to drive and she has a son at home that she'll have to break the news to. I'll grab a cab back home or something."

"Give me a call when you're ready and I'll come pick you up."

* * *

Taneka and Gina took the elevator down together. Gina told her about Harry's patient.

"Seems as though we're dealing with a lot of that kind of death right now," Taneka said. "First Carrie, then Elyse, and now this young girl."

"I don't know, Taneka, Harry's patient was a whole different story. She's a perfect example of what we try to prevent with our work. But septicemia seems like something I wouldn't expect in controlled circumstances like a clinic.

"That's true. I've worked in the department for three years and it's never happened before."

"No infections?"

"Oh, we have infections," Taneka said, "but they don't come on like these. Usually, oral antibiotics take care of them real quick. But what we've seen with Carrie and Elyse is something else. Their infections seemed to take hold with break-neck speed; by the time we got to them they were in massive organ failure."

"What do you think is causing it?"

"Well, if we used dirty instruments ... that would do the job."

Gina ignored Taneka's poor stab at humor. "But all of our instrument packs, everything, goes through the autoclave — it doesn't seem right. If it's the instruments, then someone has to be doing it deliberately.

"Who on earth would do that?" Taneka gave Gina a strange look. "I don't know you very well, Gina, but your mind works in a very weird way."

Gina laughed as they arrived on the ground floor. "You don't know the half of it."

* * *

Gina was almost late when she'd come in to work that morning; she had to park about six blocks away and run all the way to

Ridgewood in order to clock in on time. She wouldn't admit it to Harry, or anyone else, but since her accident, any heavy exertion at all left her feeling wasted. The run from her car to the hospital had practically done her in for the rest of the day.

But going home, she was grateful for the long walk. She walked with an easy pace instead of her usual frantic rush, and it gave her time to try to relax and not think about anything.

It looked like it was going to pour rain again. There were black, low-hanging clouds overhead and she could smell moisture in the air. She pulled her jacket tight around her. The minute she left the hospital, the wind picked up and now she was out-and-out cold.

There'd been no one around for the last three blocks except for a lone man walking in the same direction -- certainly not Dominick.

She'd know him anywhere.

Maybe Harry's right: I'm over-thinking that whole business.

No, she didn't believe that. She trusted her instincts; they'd saved her life too often to ignore.

She looked at the darkening sky again and picked up her pace.

Maybe it's the time of year to park the little Fiat in the underground garage at the hospital. I hate getting soaking wet.

A sense of danger prickled the hair on her neck; she turned her head around -- the man who had been walking far behind was only a step away.

He reached out to grab her and she kicked out at him. But it was too late. He'd already snagged her arm, bent it behind her, and smashed her tight up against him, so close she could smell his rank body odor and beery breath. Before she could twist away, his other hand was on her throat, choking her. She struggled, but his fingers squeezed into her windpipe and pushed up at the same time. She was forced to stand on tip toes.

"What ... do ... you want?' she croaked. "I'll give you my wallet. Let me go."

"I don't want your fucking money."

He was thin, but strong. She kept trying to pull away, but he kept shoving her toward a grungy pickup parked at the curb.

"Let me go!" She screamed every time she caught a breath.

He yanked at her arm until she thought it would break and clutched her neck even tighter until her world was spinning. He flung the truck door open.

"Get your ass in there."

She tried to resist, pushed hard against him, but she was breathless and her arm was filled with shooting pain. He half-lifted her and flung her inside. There was a sudden flash of light before blackness closed in; she barely heard him speak.

"After today, you won't be bothering my wife anymore, you bitch!"

* * *

Marvin drove to Amory's block, circled the area twice. All seemed quiet. He glanced back into the crew cab but the nosey nurse wasn't moving. Between choking her and roughhousing her into the truck, he was sure he'd done her in.

Jesus, now I gotta get rid of her?

All he could think about the past couple of days was taking out the damn nurse after Thelma told him about her and gave him a picture she'd taken with her cell phone. He'd tracked her when she left work at Ridgewood, saw where she lived. This morning, he waited near her apartment building and followed her when she left.

Everything was going his way, working out in his favor – the nurse had found a parking slot a good distance away from the hospital where there was hardly any foot traffic. And then

169

he'd found a slot for his pickup truck close to that foreign little car of hers.

Ever hear of buying American?

It had been hard to wait for her, but he'd read the newspaper from front to back, taken a couple of walks, and grabbed some fast food to pass the time. But mostly he just sat in his truck and waited.

Now that he'd taken her, the rush of excitement and the alcohol high had faded away. He suddenly saw the problem: what the hell was he going to do with her?

Shit!

He thought that if she wasn't already dead, he might finish her off right here. It wouldn't take much to choke her again. Then he could take her body to the dump.

Yeah, but what if someone sees me?

He looked at his watch – it was getting far too late for that anyway. By the time he got there, the dump would be closed for the day.

He considered hauling her to some isolated wooded area in Marin County and dumping her. Or since he didn't know Marin too good, he could find a place to throw her in the bay.

Undecided as to what course to follow, he drove to Amory's house, stopped in front, threw a blanket over the nurse, and went to the door and rang the bell.

Amory answered after a several long moments, stood in the doorway, and glared.

"What do you want, Karsh?" Amory looked Marvin up and down, then past him out to the truck. "Well?"

"I snagged the nurse."

"What nurse?"

"The one Thelma works with ... the one who might be suspicious of what's going on."

Amory looked at Marvin with steely eyes. "Where is she?"

"Out in the cab of my truck. I think she might be dead."

Amory's eyes widened. "So you brought her here? Here to *my* house?"

Marvin nodded.

"Get her out of here, you nitwit. I don't want any part of this."

"What am I gonna do with her?"

Amory leaned forward until their noses were almost touching.

"Didn't you hear me, Marvin? I don't want any part of this. Further, if I were you, I'd get rid of that nurse right now before she ends up putting you and your wife in jail. Now get out of here!"

He slammed the door in Marvin's face.

Chapter 34

Marvin was confused as he turned his back on Amory's closed door and shuffled out to the truck.

What's up with him?

Isn't he supposed to be the man in charge?

Isn't it our mission to save the lives of the unborn?

Aren't the murderers who commit the abortions and the whores who have them supposed to die?

He got into the truck, slammed the door, and turned to look under the blanket where the nurse was hidden. Even though it was almost dark, he could see that her face was pale and her lips slack. He tried to feel for a pulse the way Thelma had taught him, but her skin was cold and her hands were under her body. He couldn't bring himself to see her face while he searched for a beat on her neck.

There's nothing there.

He gave up, covered her again and started the truck.

He could see Amory watching from his living room window. The man still had a frown on his face.

Big fuckin' help you are.

Marvin decided Golden Gate Park would be the nearest safe place to dump the nurse. It was heavily wooded and most people stayed away from the area at night because of all the homeless who camped out there.

He looked down at the nurse as he started the truck. Was he sorry for what he'd done? No. He knew what was right. And he'd done the right thing.

A murderer is a murderer. This is justice.

He drove around the Richmond district until it was pitch dark, then entered Golden Gate Park at 19th Avenue. He cruised slowly through the park, looking for a place where he could pull his four-wheel drive off the paved road and into a sheltered spot. When he found what he was looking for, he backed into thick, tall bushes, killed the lights, got out, and left the door open. He was pissed at himself – no shovel, or any other tool to dig with.

Have to it with your bare hands, you knucklehead.

He reached into the crew cab, grabbed the woman under her arms, and yanked hard. She got caught up in the edge of the driver's seat at first, but when he finally pulled her free, he was almost flattened as she came tumbling out of the truck.

He bent over her sprawled body for a moment to catch his breath. He was damn tired. Tired of everything.

Now that he wasn't moving around, he heard noises in the underbrush. He couldn't tell if it was animal or human, but it didn't matter – he was spooked and didn't want to get involved with either.

He dragged the woman to one of the massive bushes that sat among tall trees; he dropped down to his knees to move aside the loose brush. It didn't take long before he reached the dirt underneath. It was hard to get any deeper than the loose stuff; after that it was hard pack. Everything he needed to help him dig was at the apartment house.

"This won't work," he muttered. "Can't get through this shit."

He pulled the nurse over to the spot he'd just cleared, turned her on her stomach, and started covering her up with the loose dirt, leaves, and pine needles he'd cleared away.

Fuck!

He remembered her purse.

Can't get caught with that.

He ran back to the truck, searched around, and finally found the purse on the floor, back under the passenger seat.

He thought about going through her wallet for money, but the noises out in the woods were scaring him.

Instead, he grabbed everything and went back to the make-shift grave. He scraped away some leaves, flattened the purse under one of her legs, and covered everything up again.

Inside the truck again, he tried to close the door as quietly as he could, but to him, the sound blasted out. Even his breathing seemed to echo back from the woods.

Gotta get the hell out of here.

* * *

Harry drove Jody's mother home in her car. She never stopped sobbing during the whole ride.

"Why couldn't she have told me?"

"Mrs. Simms—"

"Why? ... why?'

"Mrs. Simms—"

"It's Annie. Please call me Annie."

"All right, Annie. I know you're going to be asking yourself that question for a long time. And with some help, I think you'll come to terms with it. But right now you have a son who's going to need you even more than before. For his sake ... and yours ... you somehow have to get it together to help him through this tragedy, too."

"You're right, Harry ... but I don't know if I can."

Jody's family lived in the affluent St. Frances Wood neighborhood. But, as Harry had learned early on in his nursing career, wealth was never armor against tragedy. The loss of a child cut through the heart of the rich as well as the poor.

When they arrived at the Simms' home, an outside light lit the walkway up to the double-door front entrance. Harry got out and opened the passenger door.

"Would you like me to come in with you, Annie?"

"No, I think I can do this now. I have to." She touched his upper arm. "Thank you for all your help, Harry. You've been wonderful."

Harry watched Jody's mother disappear into the house.

He pulled out his cell and punched in Gina's number. She didn't answer, so he left her a message to call him. He then tried to reach Vinnie.

"Hey, Vinnie. Is Gina there?"

"You know, I was wondering about you two. Thought she was with you since she hasn't come home yet."

"I had to drive a woman home and Gina said she would come pick me up. I tried her cell, but it went to voice mail."

"Where are you?" Vinnie's voice was low and tense.

Harry gave him the address.

"I'll come get you."

Chapter 35

The sharp crunch of dry leaves and the pungent smell of mold awakened Gina. She was flat-out on her stomach and something sharp was poking her leg. She tried to take a deep breath, but her nose was clogged and she had to gasp for air through her mouth.

Her throat was closing down; she began to cough, spitting out dead vegetation from her mouth and throat.

She pushed up onto her hands and knees, scattering dirt, leaves, and twigs in all directions. She paused only a second or two before twisting around into a sitting position.

It was very dark and everything around her was drenched from the rain. When her eyes adjusted to the darkness, she could see the outlines of trees and bushes against an almost hidden sky.

Where am I?

A sudden stab of pain pierced her head and brought with it a flash of memory. A man had grabbed her off the street, forced her into a pickup truck. A blur of a face, the smells of stale beer and sweat, and ... and turpentine?

That's all she could remember.

Why had he brought her out here, half buried her in the ground? Did he think she was dead?

There was that sound again. The crunch of leaves. This time it was accompanied by the steady beat of someone walking.

She tried to retreat into a large, shaggy bush, almost certain her shuffling through the brush was too loud.

The footsteps stopped.

She froze, bit back a scream.

"Lady, are you all right?"

The voice was soft, kind, but she couldn't bring herself to respond.

"Don't be afraid ... I won't hurt you ... promise."

It wasn't him, the man who'd snatched her from the sidewalk. That, she was sure of.

"I ... I can't see you." She backed farther into the bush, then saw that her feet and ankles were still exposed.

"I'm right here in front of you, lady."

She wanted to scramble out and run.

And where are you going to run to, Mazzio?

"Are you hurt? Do you need help?"

She could hear him shuffling around someplace close to her feet.

"Take my hand. I'll help you up."

She squinted, could see a faint hand and arm moving down toward her.

She reached out and grabbed the hand, let the person lift her away from the bush. With another gentle tug, she was pulled upright. She saw then that her rescuer was an unkempt young man in dirty, scraggly clothes. Her legs were so wobbly, though, that she almost tipped over. He grabbed her by both arms and steadied her.

"Where am I?"

"Golden Gate Park."

"Someone–"

"Yeah, I know. I saw him drag you in here."

"Why didn't you call the police?" she shouted. She was hysterical and couldn't stop. "They might have caught a killer."

"Okay, lady. I get you're upset and probably mad, too, but I don't need no police comin' around here, understand? This is where I live, but the cops would drag me away. They don't like us homeless squattin' in the park." He shifted around, kicking at the leaves. "Besides, I thought you was dead, the way he was

177

draggin' you. Hell, last thing I need is to get into it with some damn killer."

Gina felt really stupid. Here was someone trying to help her and she was messing with him.

"You okay now?" He sounded worried about her.

"I think so."

"Good!" He pointed to the place where she'd been buried. "Think there may be somethin' of yours over there." He stepped away, reached down, and came up with a large and floppy object – her purse. He came back with it and hung her it on her shoulder.

That's what was poking me?

Gina rummaged inside the huge purse, searching for her cell. But a flash of memory brought back a vision of her attacker throwing it to the ground and stomping on it. Her cell was gone.

She covered her face and started to cry, hating herself for it.

"Hey, don't cry, lady. Are you looking for one of these?" He handed her an older model iPhone. "Here, you can keep it. I've got lots of them."

"You do?"

"People are always losing these suckers in the woods."

She hit the flashlight app so she could see his face and was shocked.

"Jeez, you're just a kid."

"Yeah, well kids have to live, too."

"I'm sorry ... I'm usually not this idiotic. Hey, I'm Gina ... what's your name?"

"Does it matter?"

"It matters to me."

"Look, I know the deal: I tell you my name and they come and haul me back to foster care. No way! Never again! Just call me, Dirk. That's what everyone calls me."

"Okay, Dirk. I'm going to call my fiancé and ask him to call the police ... actually an inspector I know. They'll probably come out here." She made sure he was listening to her. "Just letting you know, okay?"

He started to walk away, but Gina found her wallet, pulled out all the money she had, along with her personal card.

"This is yours, Dirk. Seventy ... seventy-two bucks. It's all I have right now. But I'm going to come back ... and find you ... and maybe there's something I can do to help you."

He took the money, rolled it up, and stashed it into a pouch that hung from his neck; he pulled another iPhone from a pocket and read her card by its light. "A nurse, huh?"

"For better or worse."

"Are you okay now, Gina?"

"I think so."

He was fidgety when he reached for her hand and shook it, but he gave her a quick smile before disappearing through the trees.

She glanced at the iPhone's clock: a little past 10:00. She punched in Harry's cell number.

Busy!

Chapter 36

Thelma was mentally exhausted. She'd lived in fear all day, worried that she might get caught by Gina Mazzio ... or someone else.

It was time to destroy her deadly cultures, move onto another way to accomplish her goal, one that wasn't so dangerous. She might infect herself ... or end up in jail ... or maybe both.

But she'd learned so much by studying about the different microbes and their silent worlds. It made her feel strong, made her want to go back to school to learn more.

She'd even mentioned it to Marvin; he'd laughed at her.

No, Marvin would never let her go back to school, even if they had the money or the time it would take. He only wanted her to do what *he* thought was important. To him, that meant continuing with what she'd started at Ridgewood, no matter what.

As for Amory, their Holy Eye leader, he wanted her to wait a little longer before she stopped using her microbes. But she still wasn't sure she could stand working around a suspicious nurse, one who might catch her in the act of contaminating the jelly. That would mean rotting in jail. The thought gave her the shivers.

Amory sent out mixed messages, seemed noncommittal. Probably didn't want anything dirty settling at his feet. Still, she liked him, and sensed that he liked her. Either way, he was a lot nicer to her than Marvin ever was.

Smells a lot better, too.

She continued preparing macaroni and cheese, Marvin's favorite dinner, other than steak. Making it from scratch was a lot of work when she could buy a box and quick-like put it together. But cooking relaxed her and she'd made enough for leftovers for tomorrow's dinner. That would be like a night off.

The smooth-as-silk white sauce was now heavily mixed with extra-sharp cheddar; it was starting to bubble and smell wonderful. She could almost taste it.

The quiet moment was fractured by Marvin crashing into the apartment.

She shoved the mac-n-cheese casserole into the pre-heated oven. He was much later than usual.

She looked across the kitchen and into the living room at her husband; her heart clenched. It wasn't the mean leer that paralyzed her, rather, it was his wet hair and clothes, covered with dirt and leaves. He looked like a drowned rat that was ready to gnaw at anything that came close to him.

"Marvin, are you all right?" She took a step in his direction. "What happened?"

He thrust a finger at her. "Don't say one more word. I'm in no mood to deal with you tonight."

Thelma retreated. Usually when he bothered to warn her to leave the room, there was a fifty-fifty chance she could get off without a beating ... if she stayed away from him, far away.

She continued to fuss with things in the kitchen until she heard him rummaging around in their bedroom.

She left the kitchen and walked quietly to the bedroom door and listened. When she heard the shower start, she stepped into the room. He'd thrown his wet clothes everywhere, her just-cleaned, white throw rug was splattered with mud and leaves.

Where has he been?

She scooped up his dirty things and tossed them into the laundry hamper. The rug looked awful, but it was too wet to deal with right now.

Thelma heard him turn off the shower.

She needed to stay out of his reach, especially when he was so volatile. She'd have to find some way to quiet him down.

She rushed back to the kitchen, looked in the oven at the mac-'n-cheese; it was starting to bubble, and the croutons on top were turning a golden brown. It would be ready in a minute. She set the table and took the salad out of the fridge.

Marvin walked in.

At least he's clean.

He looked at the food. "Is this all we're having ... salad?"

She opened the oven and pulled out the casserole. "I made your favorite dish," she said with a smile.

"Shows how fucking dumb you are. Where's my steak?"

"I thought you might like to have this tonight."

He sat down and waited for her to serve him. "Do you know where I was tonight?"

"No, dear, I don't." She kept her voice low as she spooned a heaping serving of the steaming macaroni and cheese onto his dinner plate.

"I was taking care of that nurse."

"Gina Mazzio?"

"Yeah, that's the bitch; the one you gave me a picture of."

Thelma wanted to stay calm, tried to act normal, but under the table her legs were shaking. Whatever he'd done, whatever was eating at him, it would end up being her fault.

Now, she was really frightened; her injured leg started burning. She made herself sit docilely, waited for him to take a bite before she put any food into her mouth.

"How did you find her?"

"Damn good planning." He gave her a smug smile. "Snatched her off the street, took her to Amory."

"Amory? What did he do?"

"I'll tell you what he did. He did squat! Treated me like dirt ... sent me away."

"So what did you do after that?"

He filled his mouth until his cheeks bulged.

"I got rid of her, that's what. And I did it for you! Now you can get on with our plan ... God's plan."

"Marvin, I've been thinking ... no matter what Mr. ... uh ...Amory says, we've done our part. It's getting too dangerous. The hospital's investigating those patient deaths."

"Let them look all they want. They'll never find you."

"Maybe they won't. If I stop now." She paused a beat. "I don't think Amory would mind, just so I found a different way."

"You still going on about that quitting shit?" His fork clattered onto his plate. Without warning, he leaned across the table, spilling his water glass, and grabbed her around the neck and squeezed.

"What the fuck are you talking about?" he screamed in her face. "You know that nurse, that Gina? I can plant you right next to her. Is that what you want?"

Something primal exploded inside her. She grabbed the edge of the table, pushed herself up against his hold as though her arms were made of steel. "Take your hands off me, you bastard!"

His eyes widened. He let go of her neck, pulled back a fist, and punched her in the eye.

"You ever mouth off like that again, you're dead meat. Ya hear!"

Chapter 37

Gina was angry and humiliated by the cruelty of her attacker – he'd tossed her into the truck like a useless doll, a worthless nothing. The only consolation was that he hadn't dug a hole and buried her alive.

She cinched up her soaking wet coat, but it didn't stop the water from dribbling down her neck onto her scrubs. The rain never seemed to let up, even under the umbrella of trees where she sat. With Dirk gone, loneliness encircled her; she fought against the compulsion to brush at the debris clinging to her neck – the leaves seemed to come alive, crawl up and down her skin.

It was so cold that she could barely hold still long enough to once more try the cell Dirk had given her. She knew if it had been her phone, she would have had a string of messages, all from Harry, Vinnie, and Helen. The line was still busy; she waited a moment and tried again and held her breath.

He picked up. "Harry! It's me!"

"Oh, my God, Gina! Oh, Gina, baby! Are you okay? Where are you? Can I come get you? Oh, my God, I've got to call Vinnie. He's coming apart at the seams. Tell me you're all right?"

"Other than being soaking wet, freezing to death, and having a banged up cranium, *again,* I think I'm going to make it."

"Where in hell are you?"

"Golden Gate Park."

"What are you doing there?"

"Can we fill in the details thing later? I've been buried under a pile of leaves for I don't know how long and I'm not up for talking about it right now. I just want to come home."

"Your car still at the hospital?"

"As far as I know."

"No problem. We can use can use Helen's car. Where in the park are you?"

"If I only knew. All I can tell you is that I'm surrounded by tall bushes and even taller trees. And I'm afraid that if I wander around looking for some recognizable landmark, I'll become even more lost."

"And you have no idea in which direction the nearest road might be?"

"Not a clue."

"Got an idea. Call your friend Mulzini and get the police to do their GPS thing."

"I would if I could remember his number. My cell got trashed and I'm working with one that some homeless kid gave me ... and it's close to dead."

"Check that phone for its number and I'll call it in."

She found the number and gave it to Harry. "You can try, but it's pretty late for Mulzini to still be at the police station. You could also try his personal cell and home numbers; they're in the address book in our laptop."

"I'm on it right now."

"I...I'll be h-here w-waiting, damn it." Gina's teeth started chattering so hard she could barely talk. "And, H-Harry? Please bring a dry j-jacket. I'm fr-freezing to death."

"Yeah, I caught that."

"Well, nothing's changed ... and the warmer the coat, the better."

"Don't worry. I'll take care of everything."

"Hurry, Harry. It's d-dark and I'm r-really wet ... cold ...r-really cold."

* * *

Mulzini looked at the medium-size pizza and bottle of cold beer sitting at his desk at home. He'd called the neighborhood pizzeria to deliver this big, fat, artery-clogging *Everything*. He'd even cleaned off the desktop while he waited so the box would be the center of attention. All that remained in sight was the framed picture of his wife, Marcia, who would give him holy hell if she caught him eating pizza – or anything – at this time of night.

He turned over the top of the box and, like an artist contemplating a newly finished worked, resisted touching even the outer crust.

When he could stand it no longer, he lovingly picked up a slice and took a huge bite off the pointed end. Before he could chew, his phone rang.

Who the hell?

He was on call, so he couldn't ignore it. He tried to gulp the bite in one swallow, picked up the phone, and said in an indecipherable blurt, "Hold on a minute."

He started to choke, chewed rapidly, and took big swallows of his beer, which only made things worse. He bent over and spit everything into the wastebasket. Whoever was on the other end would probably think he was nuts. He hoped it wasn't his captain.

"Sorry!"

"Hi, Inspector. Sorry to call you so late, and at home. This is Harry Lucke, Gina Mazzio's fiancé."

"Yeah, sure. Been chasing down her car accident. Gotta say I haven't found any witnesses to the Fiat's brakes being cut."

"This is something else." There was a long pause. "She didn't want to talk about it on the cell but it sounds like she was abducted earlier tonight and half-buried in Golden Gate Park."

"Jeez! You gotta be kidding. Is she all right?"

"I think so, but she doesn't know where the hell she is in the park. We were hoping you could zero in on her location with GPS."

"I have her number here. I'll do it right now."

"That won't work. Her phone was destroyed."

"Well, hell, Harry, how'd she call you?"

"Some homeless kid gave her a phone."

"Stolen, no doubt."

"Does that mean you can't zero in on her?"

"No, it's just going to take a little more work."

"I have the phone's original number, if that will help."

"Maybe it will, maybe it won't"

"Inspector, I know it's asking a lot, but I want to be there, know she's all right."

"Give me your location. I'll pick you up on the way."

* * *

Gina was curled up into a fetal position, the only way she'd found to preserve any body heat. It was so cold, she gave in to an overwhelming drowsiness and drifted off. She awoke with a start when she heard voices somewhere close by.

She sat up. Someone had placed a blanket over her, tucked it in around her. She was still cold, but she wasn't shivering and she was feeling stronger.

She watched bright lights cut through the night, highlighting the spikes of rain that continued to fall on the bushes and trees. The beams of light were heading in her direction.

"Gina! Gina!"

"Harry! I'm over here!"

It seemed to take forever to bring her legs under her to stand, but they wouldn't hold her. She toppled over.

There was a rush of feet sloughing through leaves and water, racing ahead of the glow. Then she was in Harry's arms. He was squeezing her tight against him, kissing her face, her lips.

"Baby, baby I was so scared." He held her at arms' length for a moment, then pulled her back to him. "Oh, my God!"

"I'm okay, Harry. I really am, especially now that you're here." She ran her hands up and down his body, wanting to absorb all of him. "When I was buried in those leaves, all I could think about was seeing you one more time. She threw her head back and laughed. "And breathing, of course."

"All right, you two," Mulzini said, "let's get back to reality."

"Thanks for coming. For finding me."

"So where'd you get this blanket, Gina?"

"I don't know for sure. I fell asleep, woke up with it. I think it's from the same kid who gave me the cell phone."

The paramedics interrupted as Harry was getting Gina into the heavy, East Coast winter coat he'd brought with him. They set up next to Gina. "How's it going?" one of them said. He slipped a B/P cuff on her arm. The other one went to work on her with a stethoscope.

"Look, I'm fine. I think I got clunked on the head for the second time this week, but other than freezing my ass off and getting soaked ... I'm okay."

"Let me check your head," said the EMT who had taken her B/P. He ran his fingers through her hair, used his flashlight to check her pupils. "You say you were thumped on the head again, but I can only find one spot that was recently hit. You might have had a panic or vasovagal response. That would be enough to knock you out, but I'd feel a lot better hauling you into the ER so they can give you a once over. Anyway, you know that's what the doc's going to say."

"No, I'm going home. I feel fine now. This whole thing has been a little scary, to say the least. But I want to go home."

"Babe, I think you ought to go to the ER, just to be safe."

"Safe? Harry, I feel like I'll never be safe again." She grabbed his hand. "I want to go home with you. That's where I really feel safe." She squeezed his hand hard. "Please back me up on this."

Harry stood, spoke to the two EMTs. "I'm an ICU nurse. Let the doc know I'll keep a close eye on her. She really seems to be stable."

As they packed up their gear, one of them said, "I don't think she's in any trouble now, but you know the drill -- any change, get her to the ER ... fast!"

"Damn right! Thanks."

* * *

Gina, Harry, and Mulzini sat in his car with the engine running, the heat blasting away.

The Inspector looked at her and Harry in the back seat. "How're you doing, Gina?"

"I really feel so much better now." She squeezed Harry's hand and he planted a kiss on one cheek, then the other.

"Can you tell me anything more about what happened?" The Inspector poured hot coffee from a thermos into a cup for Gina, then poured another for Harry.

"There's not much more to tell. Some guy grabbed me from behind, started choking me and threw me into a pickup, one of those with an extra seat in the back. I really don't remember anything after that until I woke up in the park, buried in a pile of dirt and leaves."

"What about his face? Do you think you could pick him out in a line-up?"

"I don't think so. It was more what he smelled like. *That*, I'll never forget."

"You told me you were worried about your ex-husband, that he may have been the one who cut your brake line." Mulzini gave out a dry laugh. "This may sound crazy, but are you absolutely sure it wasn't also him this time?"

"First of all, if it had been him, I would be dead. He would have never just left me in a pile of leaves. He would have planted me deep in the ground. Also, if it was him, don't you think I would know that?"

"Had to ask."

"I know."

"You say your cell is missing. Do you remember the guy taking it?"

"I really don't remember much of anything after he grabbed me. I think he may have stomped on it."

"First it's your brakes, then this." Mulzini poured himself a cup of coffee. He turned back and looked at Gina. "You sure as hell are on somebody's shit list."

Chapter 38

Dominick couldn't stop brooding.

There'd been real satisfaction after cutting Gina's brake line, a surge of relief, a sense of freedom. His ties to that woman were finally broken.

The reality? It had been a total failure.

What a jerk to think I finally nailed her.

Gina Mazzio, the cat woman – no matter how much I plan, no matter how much I do, she lands on her feet. Why can't I kill the bitch?

Need to move on. Need to get away from here.

The idea of moving on to Arizona stuck in his head. He thought survival there would be easier, cheaper. Certainly less crowded. He looked around the small rented room – not much better than the cell he'd occupied for three years.

Since arriving in Frisco, he'd been lonely and at loose ends. If he'd stayed in the Bronx, at least he'd know the neighborhood, have his parents close by. That would be something.

No! As long as Gina's here and alive, I'm stuck in this big, expensive, fuckin' city.

Why can't I let her go, give it up, just move on?

That same question invaded his thoughts several times a day. Yet, he knew the answer, which was simple enough: Gina Mazzio killed his baseball career.

She put him in prison.

She ruined his life.

She needed to die.

Killing her is the only way to get her out of my head ... get me out of this miserable go-nowhere city.

Lately, when not looking for Gina, he'd spent most of his time in bars drinking, looking for company. And when he was drunk, he always wanted to get into a game. He played cards or craps almost every night, with far more losses than wins. His stash of money was fast approaching zero.

He had to face reality: a measly two hundred bucks wasn't going to get him very far, or last very long if he stayed where he was. He desperately needed to get a job, line his pockets. Otherwise, he was going to be nothing but another bum on the streets of the Tenderloin.

Tacked to the wall was a picture of the Arizona desert, torn from a throwaway magazine he'd found in a bar. That had become the first thing he looked at every morning when he got up.

Arizona!

He was good with his hands and he could ace out any wetback for a gardening gig, maybe hitch onto a construction crew.

He turned away from the picture. But he wasn't going anyplace until he took care of Gina.

Gina Mazzio – the human knife that cut through his gut.

He threw a few half-hearted darts at her picture. The photo was starting to look raggedy. Her eyes and mouth had almost disappeared from being dart-stabbed so often.

Two hundred dollars. Almost broke. Shit, man! This has gotta stop!

* * *

The music was loud, giving Dominick a headache, but he sat there nursing his third beer, trying to get a buzz on. He'd let the bartender talk him into trying a local beer, Anchor, which was okay; probably better than what he usually drank back home.

A babe at the other end of the bar, the one he'd seen every night like some kind of permanent fixture, was smiling at him. Her crooked teeth needed work, but her breasts were big and she had a lot of cleavage. She seemed overdressed for a working man's bar. But, what the hell.

He lifted his beer, grabbed his change, and headed in her direction.

"Hello, beautiful."

"Hello, yourself."

He slipped onto the barstool next to her. "What are you drinking?"

"Whisky ... but a beer will do me fine."

Dominick motioned for the bartender, ordered a beer for her, another for himself.

She smiled, ran her tongue around her lips, starting a fantasy about what those lips could do. The bartender returned, set draft brews down in front of them, and flipped away the bills from in front of Dominick.

"I've seen you come in the last few nights ... alone," she said, taking a sip and leaving a moustache of foam on her upper lip.

"That right?"

Her hand slid down and around the inside of his thigh. "Call me Sonnie; that's with an *i-e*, not a *y*."

He could feel himself getting hard, but he needed to know up front if she was a pro. He didn't have the money to pay for getting laid. "You got a place nearby, Sonnie-with-an-i-e?"

"What's your hurry?"

Close-up, he could see that along with the crooked teeth, she'd had a bad case of acne and tried to cover it over with a heavy layer of makeup. It wasn't working.

He took another sip of his beer.

"What do you do to earn a buck?" he asked.

"A little of this ... a little of that."

"Uh-huh. Doing what?"

There was a long beat. "What's *your* name, fella?"

"Dominick."

"Well, Dominick, if you think I'm a workin' girl, then you got your head on backwards. I'm not a whore."

"Hey, girl!" He took her hand and put it on the rise in his pants. "I didn't think that."

"Well then, why don't we go and have us some real fun."

"We can go to my digs," Dominick said. "It ain't pretty, but it's got a bed."

Sonnie withdrew her hand, then placed it back on his thigh. "It's early ... we can go back to your place later."

"Well, whatcha got in mind?"

* * *

It was around midnight when Dominick and Sonnie stumbled down the sidewalk, headed for Dominick's room. He was wide awake, but she was having a hard time keeping her eyes open; with each step she leaned more and more into him. The heavier she leaned, the angrier he became.

Outrage was like a hot coal in his gut. He was down another hundred bucks and it was her fault. *Her* fault. Sonnie's fault! Gina's fault! Someone's goddam fault!

Somewhere along the way he finally realized that while she wasn't a whore, she *was* some kind of shill for the hole-in-the-wall basement game they went to.

She'd reeled him in like some dumb fish.

It was a quiet week night and the streets were deserted. Bums were huddled in doorways in their sleeping bags. Most of them were drunk and passed out. They didn't move a twitch as Dominick and Sonnie stumbled past. The only creatures that were alert were the dogs snuggled into their masters' sleeping bodies. Their eyes flashed and followed everyone who passed by.

When they came to an empty doorway, Dominick pulled Sonnie into it. Her eyes opened and stared into his.

"Why we stopping ... need to lie down."

When Dominick was silent, she shook herself awake. "What's the matter, baby?"

"You played me, you bitch!"

"Whadda you mean, honey."

Every muscle in his body twitched. He punched her in the mouth.

"Hey ... stop that, asshole!"

"I'll stop when I'm fucking good and ready, bitch."

Then he punched her in the belly and when she started to go down, he brought her up by the neck until she was spitting and choking, pulling at his hands, trying to pry his fingers loose.

"Just like *her* ... just like Gina ... like Gina ... like goddam Gina."

Dominick let Sonnie drop to the ground; she folded like a morning glory at noon.

A shill, that's what she is. The bitch set me up.

His hands tingled with tension as he looked around at the deserted street. He carefully pushed the woman farther back into the doorway, arranged her into a casual sitting position, allowing her head to tip forward as if she was asleep.

It was only then he felt for her pulse.

Her wrist was thin for such a full-bodied woman. He probed, searched for any sign of life. He thought he felt a soft beat, but he really didn't want to know. If she was dead, she was dead.

"Hey, man, you got some loose change?" The voice came out of nowhere; a chill zipped down Dominick's back.

He jerked around to find a bum, somewhere in his thirties to his fifties, dressed in shabby, dirty clothes. His head was tilted to one side as he looked at Dominick expectantly.

"Take a hike."

A clump of greasy hair fell across the man's forehead and his chin thrust out in belligerence. "Would it kill you to give me a fuckin' quarter?"

The street light shone on the man's face; his eyes were trying to see past Dominick to the slumped figure of Sonnie.

"Okay. Okay." Dominick reached into his pocket and came up with two quarters. "Here take these and get the hell outta here!"

The bum pocketed the money. "Is your lady okay?"

"Yeah. She's just loaded."

"She ain't moving much."

"Neither will you be if you don't get the fuck away from here." He clenched his fist, ready to slug the bum and stack him next to Sonnie.

The man backed away, looking frightened for the first time. He shuffled off down the street. When the bum staggered around the corner, Dominick took off in the opposite direction and didn't stop until he'd reached his room.

He collapsed on the bed, exhausted. He couldn't even raise an arm to set the alarm clock so he could get up early the next morning.

When Dominick finally awoke, it was after ten a.m.

He lay in bed until he was wide awake, thinking about the events of the night before. Was Sonnie alive or dead? Cold sweat trickled down from his arm pits, fear washed over him.

"Oh, shit,' he muttered.

He forced himself to sit up, look around, and take in his surroundings. Only the rough-torn picture of the Arizona desert and the dart-punctured photograph of Gina on the back of the door gave the room any personality. The ragged parts of what was left of her face taunted him. He closed his eyes to try to stop the hatred for her that repeatedly bubbled over him like dirty storm water.

Nothing stopped it.

If Sonnie was dead, it was Gina's fault. All she ever did was fuck up his life.

He had to think. Had to forget Gina and get out of San Francisco. He was never going back in the joint, and if he stayed here, that was where he would end up. That or dead.

He pulled his duffel bag from the closet and set it up on the bed. It took less than five minutes for him to empty the drawers and pack up.

He checked his wallet. Eighty dollars ... and he owed the landlord forty of it.

Well, fuck that! I'm out of here. The greasy bastard will just have to suck it up, swallow the loss. No way will he ever find me in Arizona.

It made him feel weird, his head all crazy and muddled to leave without finishing what he'd set out to do. He'd only come to Frisco to put an end to Gina, once and for all.

He grabbed a piece of paper from the small notebook he always carried on him. He planned to leave a note on the windshield of her stupid car. He wanted to let the bitch know that he'd been here, and that he wasn't finished with her.

Not by a long shot.

There was so much he wanted to write, but he merely scribbled, in dark, heavy print:

Don't get too comfortable.

Chapter 39

"One day you're going to stop pushing yourself so hard," Harry said, sipping the last of his morning coffee. "Would it be so terrible if you took a day off after all that happened last night?"

Gina had just put on her makeup and was getting a jacket from the closet. She would never admit it to Harry, but she was still shaky and couldn't seem to get warm enough. "Would you love me if I was any other way?"

"You know I love you, no matter what kind of nut you are."

She gave him a wide smile. "Think I'll try to find a closer parking place from now on, and on a different street." She laughed. "Might even try the hospital garage, if they'll let me in. In fact, wish I'd put the Fiat in there yesterday ... not too happy about it being out there on the street overnight, then all day today."

"We can ask Helen and Vinnie to take a swing by your parking space this morning to see if your baby is okay, if we have time. Then you can pick it up when you get off work, like you always do. And if my shift ends on time, maybe I can walk with you, sort of like your personal bodyguard."

"That would be nice." She sighed. "Yeah, just the two of us. That way I'll have an excuse to fend off Vinnie, who's going to want to hover over me, watch my every move."

"You're not sounding all that confident about the day, doll. I mean, would it hurt to lie back for a day? Stay home, get yourself together? I mean, I'd promise to bring the Fiat straight home ... not harm it in any way."

"You're a nut, Harry Lucke. But I do feel pretty good. Besides, you know I can't take more time off. The unit is short-handed and I don't want to lose this job."

"They're not going to fire you for taking a sick day, especially when you were kidnapped, for crissake, and buried in the park."

"Maybe I should tell Taneka it was Captain Hook and he was going to come back for me and whisk me off to Neverland."

"You're impossible."

"I'm going back to work, Harry. Accept it, okay?" She took his hand, pulled him closer, and kissed his cheek. "Besides, it isn't only missing a day of work."

"What is it?"

"That man who attacked me?"

"Yeah."

"In the middle of the night, I remembered something he said when he threw me into his truck."

"I didn't know he'd said anything."

"He said, 'After tonight, you won't be bothering my wife anymore, you bitch.'"

"Do you know this guy's wife?"

"Don't even know him, but I've been giving it some serious thought."

"Love ... we just got back from Nevada, you've hardly had a chance to meet anyone new."

"That's my point, Harry. It would have to be someone connected with Women's Health."

"Maybe."

"No maybes about it. The only person I can think it might be is Thelma."

"Her again?"

"She's accused me of spying on her."

"Are you?"

"Actually, I wasn't at the time. But that woman's up to something. And we have two dead women as a result of having abortions in our clinic."

"Why would Thelma want to hurt those women, any women?"

"Haven't the slightest idea," Gina said. "For all I know, maybe she's one of those anti-abortion fanatics."

"If that were the case, why would she take a job in Women's Health in the first place?"

Harry looked at Gina with a certain expression, the one she'd come to know meant he was scrutinizing everyone and everything. "Then again, maybe she's nosing around under cover – a nut case against abortion in sheep's clothing."

"Funny," Gina said, "that was exactly my thought."

* * *

Gina and Harry were at the curb waiting for Helen and Vinnie to pick them up for a ride to Ridgewood. When Helen's bright red Prius pulled up and double-parked in front of the apartment house, Vinnie was out the door instantly, grabbing Gina and pulling her into his arms.

"Are you sure it wasn't Dominick?" he blurted, hugging her. "I'll hunt down the bastard and kill him if he laid one finger on you."

She gently tried to pull back, but he wouldn't let go. "As I told you last night, I'm all right, Vinnie. Really I am. And after some sleep and my morning coffee, I'm still sure it wasn't Dominick."

"Hey man, she's okay," Harry said, squeezing Vinnie's shoulder.

Helen was leaning against the car, a weak smile on her face. Gina could see that she, too, was beat.

"Vinnie didn't sleep all night," Helen said. "He paced back and forth ... couldn't stop talking about you ... what it was like after your ex beat you ...the hospital, surgery, then it was Afghanistan ... the bombs, the noise. He couldn't stop."

Gina gave her brother a tight hug. "Hey, guy, I'm here and I'm fine." She put her hands on either side of his face, looked squarely into his eyes. "Pay attention: I'm fine ... honestly."

"Gina just happened to be in the wrong place at the wrong time and this nut grabbed her," Harry said. "But everything's okay now."

* * *

The two women got into the car – Helen in the driver's seat, Gina next to her. As Vinnie opened the back door to get in, Harry gently tugged at his arm.

"Listen, Vinnie. I've got a close friend who works with vets who have the same kind of problems you're having. He's an amazing guy."

"I'm not going to some shrink, man. I'll get over this."

"No, you won't." Harry's voice turned hard. "You need help ... and you need it now!"

Vinnie's face flushed; before he could refuse again, Harry said, "I don't want to be rough on you, man. You're Gina's brother, a great guy, and all that. But you're scared ... and stressed. It seems to be getting worse every day." He grabbed Vinnie by both arms. "And you know it."

Vinnie tried to pull away, but Harry held onto him until he stopped struggling. Vinnie said in a soft whisper, "Even with Helen, I can't stop it! The things I see ... everything is horrible. I'm scared all the time. So bad sometimes, I just want to run and run and never stop until I drop."

Harry looked him square in the eyes. "I'll go to the doc with you ... I'll be there every step of the way." He wrapped an arm around Vinnie, grasped him as tight as he could. "I promise."

Vinnie collapsed. He threw an arm over Harry's shoulder and held onto him as if his life depended on it. Harry lowered him onto the car seat and went around to the other side.

"I don't think he should go into work today," Harry said. "Maybe we should take him back to your place, Helen."

"No! No need," Vinnie protested. "I can shake it off."

"This isn't good, Vinnie," Gina said. She leaned over her seatback and put a hand on his knee. "Come on, let's take you up to our apartment. We're right here, already."

Vinnie slowly shook his head from side to side. "Let's get going before we're all late," he said. "I've pushed it all back inside where it belongs." He put a hand on top of Gina's. "You can check me out again, sis, when we get to Ridgewood."

Chapter 40

"I'm still not sure Vinnie should be going to work today," Harry said.

"Likewise, but there was no arguing with him," Gina said.

When the elevator reached her floor, she slipped her arm out of Harry's grasp and whispered in his ear, "I love you, Harry Lucke." She stepped out of the car and left him behind with a couple of bemused medical assistants.

Walking down the hall, weariness hit her like a sledge hammer. She couldn't remember ever having been so tired, and so sore all over. It felt like her bones might poke holes in her skin at any moment.

Harry was right: she should have stayed home.

One day I'm going to learn not to be so stubborn.

She took a trio of deep breaths to pull herself together, glanced at her watch as she rounded a corner and slammed into Thelma Karsh. Every part of her cried out in pain.

Thelma looked at her in wide-eyed confusion. "Um ... er ..." Thelma stammered, "my fault ... didn't mean it."

Before Gina could respond, the medical assistant dashed away.

Gina rubbed hard at her shoulder where they'd crashed together.

Now that was weird, really weird.

* * *

Thelma was breathless as she hurried on down the corridor. Her heart wrenched, she had to slow down.

She's alive! My God, she's still alive.

Marvin said she was dead; she's supposed to be dead.

203

What if she remembers Marvin's face? Can't ever let her see Marvin and me together. Never!

Thelma rubbed at her bruised neck where Marvin's thumbs had almost choked the life out of her.

My own husband almost killed me.

Now she wished he had.

If they picked him up, he would scream the truth out to anyone who would listen. He would tell them how he and his wife had delivered justice for the unborn.

Everyone would know then that she was a murderer.

She would go to prison for the rest of her life.

* * *

Frannie Garrity was angry. Ryan refused to try to change a new student's mid-day piano lesson; she'd been equally adamant in refusing to change her doctor's appointment. That evolved into a terrible fight about money, bills, commitment, and everything else that was going wrong. Instead of resolving any of it, the situation between them got worse.

He didn't cancel the lesson and she'd gone to the Ridgewood Women's Health Center ... alone.

After registering, Frannie slid into a seat in the clinic reception area. Several women were sitting in chairs all around her. They looked as nervous as she felt.

She kept going over everything again and again. She could see no possible way that she could keep this pregnancy.

If she did, she was certain they'd be living in their car with the twins in the not too distant future. So that was that.

"Frannie Garrity?"

She stood so quickly her purse dropped to the floor. She felt like an idiot as she scooped it up, almost losing her balance in the process.

"I'm here," Frannie said. In her rush to get inside, she turned an ankle and almost fell. The person at the door started toward her, but she waved her off and bent over to rub at the pain. She took a deep breath, stood upright, and wiggled the foot. It seemed to be okay, but now she knew everyone in the waiting area was focused on her.

Okay, so I'm their entertainment for the day.

She forced herself to continue on without looking around at the others, and then gave a weak smile to the medical assistant, who was still holding the door for her.

"Mrs. Garrity, my name is Thelma. I'm one of the medical assistants in the department. Would you please come with me?"

Her formal tone brought Frannie to attention. There was something off-putting about her.

Maybe she's having a bad day, too. Mine certainly hasn't been all that great so far.

When they reached a small examination room, Thelma preceded her inside and immediately went to a tray next to the exam table.

"Take your clothes off from the waist down and sit on that table."

Frannie was surprised by the assistant's attitude, which had gone from formal to gruff, to rude. Being an artist, Frannie tended to study just about any person she came in contact with. She took them in from the head to toe – all were fair game.

Frannie stared at the medical assistant's name tag, then at her dark, gray-striped mess of hair. Deep frown lines etched the woman's face; this was not a happy person. Yet, there was also an aura of excitement ... no ... agitation. And there was no mistaking a strong undercurrent of permanent anger that emanated from her like heat from a radiator.

Thelma's attitude was just a reminder of how badly things had gone since she'd become pregnant. Anything that could go haywire would go haywire. Everything, including her relationship with Ryan, was screwed up. Even the simplest of things were no longer simple, including the way she was being treated by this medical assistant.

"Is there something wrong?" Frannie demanded. She could feel her phony smile, a pasted-on Halloween mask of teeth, spread across her face.

Thelma ignored her, acting very busy as she placed a square of paper with jelly on it and a speculum on the tray. She used a cotton applicator to stir the jelly. She stared at Frannie, her eyes narrowed like a viper's.

"Why don't you sit down and not worry about my state of mind?"

"Hey, you!" Frannie shouted, leveling a finger to point at Thelma. "You don't get to talk to me like that!"

"And you don't get to be so rude to me," Thelma responded.

"Get out of here!" Frannie shouted.

Thelma's jaw dropped, but she stood rooted in one spot.

"I don't want you in here with me," Frannie yelled even louder. "Get out! Now!"

Chapter 41

Dieting was out, eating well was in.

That was Gina's mantra, at least until she felt stronger. A full lunch of vegetable-ladened minestrone soup, that didn't even remotely come close to tasting Italian, plus a grilled cheese sandwich, left her stuffed and calorie sated.

It was rare that she ate by herself in the hospital cafeteria, but Harry couldn't make it and she didn't push for lunch with Helen and her brother. Vinnie probably needed some time away from her. Gina understood that. She also knew he was emotionally wasted and she wouldn't rest until the Vinnie she'd always known was back again.

It hurt, but Gina had to face the facts: maybe *that* Vinnie, *that* person, was gone forever. The fun-loving brother she used to know had changed, morphed into a man burdened with the pain and terrors of having gone to war ... too many times. Thinking about it made her want to cry. But Harry had promised to watch over Vinnie, and he never made a promise he couldn't keep. That was her Harry.

Between thoughts of her brother, Thelma's face kept popping into her head. Gina could still see the look on her face when they'd run into each other earlier. It was as though Thelma had seen a ghost.

* * *

Back in the unit, Gina watched Thelma bring in a patient for an examination. She wondered why Thelma was so strange, why she usually acted so antagonistic around her. She wanted to ask questions about Thelma's husband, but she knew better than to be *that* blatant.

Maybe I need to stop trying to read things into her behavior. Maybe she's simply strange, and that's all there is to it.

No, I've known a lot of off-beat people. This is beyond that. Something's eating at her. There's no getting around it. She acts like she's guilty of something, like she's doing something wrong.

I know guilt when I see it.

She recalled the time Thelma jumped all over her when she thought she'd been overheard in an examination room-conversation between her and a patient.

All that craziness with the KY jelly. What's with that? And why the culture pack in her pocket when they're stocked in every patient examination room?

It made no sense, unless there really was a direct connection between the culture tube and the KY jelly.

When Gina mentioned it to Taneka, the supervisor agreed that it was odd since medical assistants didn't take cultures of any kind in the unit. The conversation went no further.

But Thelma's definitely up to something

.

* * *

"I don't want you in here with me!" echoed down the hall. Gina ran toward the examination room where the shouting was coming from.

"Get out of here! Now!"

Gina pushed open the door. A patient was standing at the end of the table yelling at Thelma, who turned to Gina with confusion written all over her face.

"Is there a problem?"

The patient eyed Gina. "Yes, there is definitely a problem. I don't want her in here." The woman wiped at tears running down her cheeks. "It's bad enough I have to have an abortion ... I don't need to be reminded of it ... treated like dirt ... by *that* woman." She raised her arm and pointed at Thelma.

"Maybe you'd better go," Gina said quietly to Thelma. "Let me handle this."

Thelma merely nodded. As she turned to leave the room, she reached out to scoop up the paper square loaded with KY jelly.

"Leave that!" Gina said. "Leave everything just as it is!"

Thelma hesitated for only an instant before hurrying out the door.

The patient was sobbing. "It's not like I want to be here. I wish I didn't have to do this ... but I have to ... I have to."

Gina took the patient's arm, smoothed her hair, spoke gently to her. "I'm sure it's only a misunderstanding."

"No! That woman was judging me ... treated me like a thing ... like I wasn't human."

Gina glanced at the computer screen, saw the patient's name. "Let's get you undressed, Mrs. Garrity, so the doctor can examine you."

"Fine. But I don't ever want to see *her* again." She pointed, this time at the now-closed door.

Gina helped her off with her clothes, seated her on the end of the table with the drape on her lap. "Just let me finish getting things ready and the doctor will be in soon. Then you can be on your way. Okay?"

Gina took Thelma's KY jelly, topped it with another square of paper, and carefully put it in a plastic bag. No time like the present to find out if there were any bad bugs in the Thelma's lavish portion.

Of course, if Taneka finds out what I've done, I'll catch hell, but it won't be the first time ... and I may get some evidence that the KY is a contributing factor to the two post-abortion deaths

She squeezed out a fresh, smaller glob of jelly for the exam, turned to Frannie Garrity, and said, "Are you all right now?"

"I'll feel a lot better when this is over and I'm out of here."

Chapter 42

Frannie Garrity cried throughout the examination; she wouldn't let go of Gina's hand the whole time. When it was over, it took Gina a long time to quiet her down. Then, after scheduling her appointments, and assuring her that she would be with her during the procedures, Gina saw her out. She rushed off to the workroom to use the department microscope. She was so excited, so certain she would find something suspicious that she had trouble getting the door shut

She took Thelma's KY jelly from her pocket, used an applicator to smear a thin layer onto a slide, and topped it with a cover glass. Placing it under the scope, she used different magnifications to see if the pathogens she suspected were actually in the specimen.

But all she saw was a whole lot of artifact, a few stray bacteria, and some strands of yeast.

She was disappointed, but it didn't really surprise her. She'd known the only definitive way to see if there was any strep present would be to plate it out. She'd had to try, though.

"What are you doing?" Thelma's voice cut through Gina's thoughts as she strained to look at the slide one more time.

The medical assistant was standing in the doorway, hands on hips, looking like a gorilla ready to pounce.

"Frankly, it's none of your business, Thelma."

"Is that KY Jelly you took from the tray I set up?"

"And what if it is?"

The woman was fuming. "You embarrassed me."

"You embarrassed yourself upsetting a patient so much that she was forced to order you out of the room."

"This isn't over," Thelma said, her whole body trembling.

"Damn straight," Gina said to her retreating back.

211

Gina removed the slide and threw it into the wastebasket. She took a fresh culture tube and grabbed a sample from the remaining batch of KY Jelly and entered her own patient number and name before shipping it off to the lab.. One way or another she intended to find out if there were any pathogens present.

Thelma was very smart or very dumb, but either way, Gina was going to get the information. She didn't want to think about what might happen if the KY did carry deadly microbes and she could tie them to Thelma. And what if that *was* Thelma's husband who had attacked her? And what if Thelma told him I was suspicious of her?

Well, she'd have to deal with all that one step at a time.

* * *

"What's this all about, Gina?" Taneka said, an eyebrow climbing skywards. "Are you accusing Thelma of something unethical?"

"I think she's contaminating the KY Jelly ... deliberately."

"That's the dumbest thing I've ever heard." Taneka was really angry. "Supposing, I mean, just supposing she would do a thing like that. Why? For what possible reason?"

"It might have something to do with her being against abortion."

"Oh, for God's sake, do you hear yourself? She's been working here for three years. Why would she even hire on to Women's Health if she was against abortion? Besides, I think I would have picked up on something like that a long time ago."

"Maybe, maybe not."

"Thelma has been one of our best workers ... and that includes the RNs who float through here and then disappear like

212

a bad memory." Taneka tapped her pen with every word. "She's here reliably, and she works hard."

"I'm just saying ... she might not be the person you think she is. We've had two post-abortion deaths in a very short period of time. We should be looking at everything, don't you think?

"Coincidences do happen."

"Do you really believe that, Taneka?"

"I believe it's possible. And what makes you think Thelma is against abortions anyway. Have you seen anything to indicate that?'

"There's just something about the way she acts with patients ... and they seem to pick up on it."

"I mean, why would she wait three years to act out if she was a pro-lifer? That simply doesn't make sense to me."

Gina had no answer, couldn't come up with a response ... at least not at present.

* * *

Thelma saw Taneka and Gina sitting at the desk in the nurses' station as she came down the hallway. They were talking, heads only a few inches apart..

I wonder what that bitch is saying to Taneka.

Taneka motioned for her to come closer.

"Hi, Thelma," Taneka said in her usual friendly tone. "Come and have a seat."

Thelma sat down in one of the chairs. She grabbed a quick glance at Gina – saw her mouth was clamped shut; she looked tense and unyielding.

"Gina tells me one of the patients was very angry with you this afternoon."

Before Thelma could respond, Gina said, "She screamed for Thelma to get out of the room."

"What happened?" Taneka asked.

Thelma knew her job depended on how she handled herself the next few minutes; she also knew it was her word against Gina's, unless they decided to question the patient, Frannie Garrity. "I don't know what happened. I'd just roomed her and for no reason she became extremely emotional and began shouting at me to get out."

"Why do you suppose the patient felt that way?" Taneka said in a quiet voice.

"All I can figure is that like most women in her position, she was very emotional. I must have upset her in some way."

"What position is that?" Gina demanded.

Thelma felt herself flush. "Uh ... you know ... someone about to have an abortion."

"That have anything to do with your special handling of the KY Jelly?"

"I don't know what you're talking about, Gina," Thelma said with a slight smirk. "That sounds pretty silly."

Gina's eyes bored holes through her.

"I suppose it does, but you seem to use an awful lot of the stuff."

Thelma forced herself to laugh. "I didn't know there was a shortage, or a designated amount we were supposed to use."

Gina appeared flustered and Thelma could also see that Taneka was not happy with this whole line of questioning. "I don't know what you're talking about, Gina. I always try to take care of the doctors and give them what they need. What have I done wrong?"

"Why were you carrying a portable culture tube pack?" Gina said.

"Well ... I usually carry one in my pocket in case the doctor wants to take a culture ... why else?"

"Even when they're stocked in the drawers of every examination room?"

"That's enough!" Taneka said. "Okay, Thelma, thanks for being so patient ... go on back to what you were doing."

* * *

"Are you satisfied now, Gina?"

"Well—"

"—well, nothing. I felt like a perfect idiot asking those questions of Thelma," Taneka said. "I did it because you're a colleague, and I try to be fair when this kind of situation arises. But I don't like to be made a fool—"

"—I didn't," Gina interrupted.

"—Thelma has been a valued employee with an outstanding record for the past three years and suddenly you step in and malign her. Why?"

"I'm just trying to get to the bottom of our contamination problem."

"At Thelma's expense? Besides, I'm not even convinced we have a contamination problem here."

"I'm sorry if I embarrassed you. I'm only trying to help."

Taneka gave Gina a long, speculative stare. "I must say, I haven't been totally impressed with you, Gina. If we keep having problems like this, I'm afraid I won't be able to keep you in the department."

"But—"

"—but, nothing! Am I making myself clear, Gina?"

"Yes, Taneka, you are."

Chapter 43

Inspector Mulzini checked his notes to verify his exact location in Golden Gate Park. Yeah, this was the place where they'd picked up Gina Mazzio.

Everything looked different in the light of day. At night, the scattered headlight beams had created more eerie, shadowy corridors, but this was definitely the place. Besides, his GPS wouldn't lie.

He pulled up to the side of the road and looked around several times, still not convinced that this was the right spot.

Have to start somewhere.

He got out of the car and walked to the edge of the tree line. The woods were particularly thick here and he felt an edge of concern again as he walked through the forest with his inner antennae on alert. Last year, one of the Inspectors from his division was found dead somewhere around here. He was pretty sure it was in this general area.

Mulzini remembered the Inspector had failed to call in his location, and no one could figure out what made him go nosing into this particular neck of the park. The guy had been one of those unpopular cops, which led to a lot of speculation that he might have gone rogue. Trafficking in drugs was high on the rumor list. Since no one was ever collared, department gossip had messed up the cop's reputation in an underhanded way that Mulzini didn't like.

Walking through the trees, the pungent odors of eucalyptus, mold, and damp leaves reminded him how he used to spend his free time camping. When he was a kid, his father would take him to all the national parks in the area, always challenging him to walk softly and silently, to become one with the environment.

216

After a while, he could actually sneak up on wandering deer and surprise them. It was spooky how they never bolted, as Mulzini expected. They would majestically glide away and move deeper into the forest.

From one step to the next, he was out of the sunlight and into the dark shadows of an uninterrupted ring of trees. There wasn't a sound to be heard, a movement to be seen.

He found the spot where Gina had been buried in leaves. Signs of the shallow grave were still evident. Not really a grave, more a hasty cover up. Whoever had dumped her here probably was unprepared to deal with a dead body.

The leaves and pine needles crunched under foot as he circled the area.

When he stopped and stood still for a moment he could pick up faint sounds coming from deeper into the woods. He moved silently in that direction, trying to blend in with the natural environment. His instincts put him on special alert, mindful again of the unsolved crime of the dead Inspector.

He pulled out his gun and moved forward, slipping behind tree trunk after tree trunk. Whatever was making the noise was farther away than he'd first thought. It took him a few minutes of stealth walking before he came on two figures arguing. He dropped to his knees and crawled ahead carefully.

"Get away from me or I'll stick this knife in you."

The speaker was a teenager and about half the size of the man he was threatening, who appeared to be in his thirties.

"Remember the last time you tried this shit?" the boy said, waving the knife back and forth in front of him.

"Why don't you get it, kid? I ain't gonna hurt ya." The man took a step closer. "Just gonna warm you up. Probably been freezing your ass off out here."

The boy took a step back. His legs were visibly shaking. Mulzini knew how the rest of this was going to turn out if he didn't step in.

The Inspector stood up behind the bush he'd been using for cover. "Leave the kid alone!" he yelled and stepped forward.

"What the fuck do—" The man saw the gun in Mulzini's right hand, the badge in the left. "Hey, man. I don't want no trouble over a piece of ass." He suddenly turned tail and disappeared in the woods. The boy tried to get away, too, but Mulzini latched onto one arm and held tight.

"Please, sir. Please let me go," he said, sounding like a character out of *Oliver Twist*.

"It's okay. Take it easy." Mulzini holstered his gun. "I just want to ask you a few questions. That's all."

"You'll let me go then?"

"Let's talk first." Mulzini wouldn't let go of the arm.

"What do you want?"

Mulzini pointed back in the direction from which he'd come. "A woman was found over there recently. Do you know anything about it?"

The boy's face drooped. "Did she tell you about me? She promised she wouldn't say nothin' to nobody." He tried to pull his arm free again.

Mulzini tightened his grip. "Gina didn't even mention you, kid. I just came back to check things out and heard you with that creep."

"Yeah, he's been tryin' to get into my pants for a year now. Been havin' to change my hideout." The kid turned away. "It's getting' harder and harder to get away from the bastard."

"That how long have you been on the streets?"

"I'm not on the streets ... I'm in the park."

The kid was getting to him. Mulzini could see he'd been trying to stay clean. But not succeeding too well – his neck was grubby with rings of dirt and while his hands appeared clean, every fingernail was black with grunge. Mulzini looked at his clothes and sleeping bag. They were stained from top to bottom. The only plus was a scattering of books near a small, draw-string tote bag.

"What's your story, anyway?" Mulzini asked.

"What's it to you? Like, if you're thinkin' of taking me in and calling my parents, forget it. I haven't got no one who wants me around, so do whatever you think you have to do."

The kid was putting up a good front, and trying to be a smart-ass, but the Inspector knew there were tears working their way to the surface.

When did I turn into such a soft touch?

"Let's forget about you for a moment."

"Dirk."

"What?"

"That's my name, Dirk."

"Okay, Dirk. I'm Inspector Mulzini. If I let go of your arm will you stay put?"

"Yes, sir."

"You're not just jiving me, are you?"

"No, sir. I give you my word."

How many times have I heard that bullshit?

Mulzini let go of Dirk's arm, ready for a chase at any moment, but the kid seemed to be a straight-shooter. He didn't run.

"Did you see a man drag a woman into this area, cover her up in leaves?"

Dirk nodded. "I saw Gina, yeah. Gave her a telephone to call the cops."

"Yeah, she told me a little bit about you."

Mulzini watched the muscles of Dirk's face contract in anger.

"Listen, kid, Gina didn't squeal on you, if that's what you're thinking. Didn't say a word about what you looked like, or in which direction you went after you left her. *I* found you by accident. She kept her word.

That seemed to quiet the boy. The Inspector could only guess how many people had let this kid down over the years.

"Did you see anything else, Dirk?"

The boy started an in-place walk. His moving feet seemed to warm him up and help him think. "I saw it all."

"That so? What happened?"

"Well, this guy drives up in a white crewcab ... backs right into the woods 'til he can't drive no more. Gets out, pulls Gina from the back seat, tries to dig a hole with his hands. But that ain't happenin, so he gives it up. Then he covers her over with leaves and stuff."

"You saw all of that?"

"Yes, sir. Then I followed him back to his truck. The guy was spooked. You'd have thought ghosts were chasin' him."

"Did you see anything else?"

"Yeah, he drove out of here like a scared rabbit."

Mulzini paced back and forth before he stopped in front of the kid again. The two of them just stood, staring into each other's eyes.

"Are you looking to get off the streets?"

"Inspector, you've been square with me, so I'll say right out, I'm not goin' back to any foster care dump. I mean, you can drag me in and I won't fight you, but at the first opp, I'll be gone."

"I hear you, Dirk. But suppose I could get you into a place ... a friend of mine runs a home for kids like you."

"Yeah, sure."

"I've sent three kids to him before and if he likes you, he'll take you in."

"Take me in?"

He placed a hand on the boy's shoulder. "Let's just say if you're not happy there, we'll make sure you never have to camp out again ... no matter what."

The boy sat down on the ground. He was silent until his skinny body began to shake. Soon he was bawling his eyes out.

"Hey, Dirk," Mulzini said rubbing the boy's shoulder. "It's okay ... let's try to make things better." He helped Dirk to his feet. "We'll stash you at my house until we can get things together. My wife will love having you around ... our kids are grown and gone, and so far, no grandkids."

Dirk looked at him. "You mean it?"

The Inspector smiled, holding back a tear or two of his own. "Grab your stuff and let's get out of here."

The boy ran to his sleeping bag, gathered up his stuff, and rolled it all up together.

Once they were inside Mulzini's car, Dirk said, "There's one thing I forgot to tell you, Inspector."

"Hey, call me Mulzini, that's all anyone ever calls me."

The boy smiled at him. "When the man who brought Gina ... you know, like when he turned to leave ... I saw there was some kinda sign on the door of his truck."

"A sign? You mean like the name of a business ... something like that?"

"Yeah."

"Well? What did it say?"

"It was hard to read, but I think it said somethin' like Katt's Apartment Management, you know?"

Chapter 44

When Thelma came home from work, the apartment was shadowy and still. Marvin was obviously out, either working or maybe fooling around.

Where is he?

A thread of suspicion that he was sleeping with one of the tenants in the building grew into a slash of hatred when she walked into the bedroom. The floor was a mess of his discarded dirty clothes. Of course, *she* was expected to take care of them.

He never dressed up for anyone, yet when she looked in the closet, one of his two decent sport shirts was missing – the one she liked best. Fuming, she kicked his dirty, discarded clothes from one end of the room to the other. Finally, she bent down and picked up an armful.

Who does he think he is to cheat on me, give himself to some other woman?

She stomped into the kitchen and dumped the dirty bundle on the table.

Let him fix his own dinner. And clean up his own crap.

"I won't be treated like this anymore. I won't," she screamed at the kitchen walls.

She sat down at the kitchen table, shoved his dirty clothes aside, laid her head into her arms, and wept.

* * *

Thelma looked at the kitchen clock when she heard Marvin come in, whistling some off-key tune. It was after seven. He slammed the door shut and continued whistling; she sat up tall at the table, waiting to confront him. She was overwhelmed with a sense of hatred.

"What're you looking at, woman?"

"You!" She could see a smudge of lipstick on his collar.

"Well, stop it!" He stuck a finger into the pile of dirty clothes. "What's with this shit, and where the hell is my dinner?"

"Let the bitch you've been sleeping with feed you."

A grimace of anger crossed his face. "What the fuck are you talking about?"

"Who is she?"

He stared at her a moment more before throwing his head back and roaring with laughter. "What's with you? You finally gone off your rocker?"

"That's all you have to say?" She pointed, moving a finger up and down his length. "Look at you ... all dressed up. You don't do that for me ... ever."

He walked around the table as though he was strolling in the park and suddenly reached out, grabbed her by the hair, and yanked her out of her chair. "Who the hell do you think you're talking to with that nasty mouth of yours?"

"I'm talking to you!" She spit in his face. "I won't stand for it, you hear me?" She pulled at his fingers, trying to loosen his grip, but he only clutched her hair tighter. Spittle ran down his cheek.

"If I want to fuck someone else, that's what I'll do. And you better remember that."

"No, you won't, Mr. Big Shot. I'll not only leave you, I'll go to the police, tell them what you've been doing."

His mouth hung open in surprise. "You're about as dumb as they come," he said, laughing at her again. "You're the one making up that mess of goo. You're the one killin' those women, not me."

She screamed in his face. "If you think you're out of this, you're not so smart yourself."

He threw her against the table; she rolled off the edge and fell to the floor.

"What are you talking about?"

Thelma got up, rubbed her ribs, and plopped down in a chair. She was so angry she barely felt the pain. "You said you killed that nurse, Gina Mazzio."

"Yeah, I took care of her. So?"

"So why was she at work today? Almost caught me messing with the KY jelly."

"Bullshit!"

"I guess I was talking to a ghost."

His eyes went dull. "I buried the bitch in Golden Gate Park ... she was dead ... wasn't breathing."

"*You* thought she wasn't breathing? Well, I'm here to tell you, Marvin Karsh, you're obviously not smart enough to know when someone is or isn't breathing. Gina Mazzio was at work today, no worse the wear for *your* bumbling efforts."

"But—"

"—but nothing, you fool. And remember, since you're the one who tried to kill her, who do you think she'll point a finger at?"

He smacked her hard across the face. She reached up to cover the burn with her palm.

"You better do what you're supposed to," he said. "We're in this together."

She snatched a t-shirt from the dirty clothes, wiped lipstick off his cheek, showed it to him, and threw it in his face.

"And *you* better not forget that the next time you dare to mess around with some floozy."

Chapter 45

"Gina, you don't really *know* it was your ex-husband," Mulzini said. "It was a note. Anyone could have written it and left it on your windshield."

"Inspector, I *know* it was him," she said into her cell phone.

"How can you be so sure?"

"My brother Vinnie made some calls back East – checked around our old Bronx neighborhood." Gina had to swallow hard to keep from screaming at Mulzini. "Dominick took off ... broke parole." She looked out the window. Rain had started pouring down.

"Okay, okay, let me think about this, Gina. I've got s few other things I'm looking into."

"You're not just putting me off, are you?"

"You know me better than that."

Gina didn't respond for a moment. When she did, her voice was tight. "People change, Inspector."

* * *

"But it was on my car." Gina gave the *Don't-get-too-comfortable* note to Harry, then resumed her pacing back and forth between the sofa and window. "First Mulzini won't listen, now it's you."

"Look, doll. Mulzini is a professional. He's not going to chase after hunches."

"Okay, but why won't *you* believe me? It *has* to be Dominick. Like, who else?"

"Maybe it was the guy who kidnapped you and tried to bury you in the park."

Gina shook her head, tried to calm herself, but fear rumbled deep inside her. "I told you ... told you he was here ... that he was the one who cut my brake lines."

Harry caught her arm, looked into her eyes. "Come on, doll. Please calm down. Just because Dominick broke parole and no one has seen him for awhile, that doesn't mean he's in San Francisco. Besides, regardless of where that creep is, you and I ... we'll work it out."

"Don't tell me to calm down, Harry. I can't do it. You weren't the one married to that maniac." She yanked her arm away. "It was *me*."

"Gina Mazzio, don't you dare pull away from me. I'm always on your side. *Always*."

"Don't you get it? I feel so trapped. There's this crazy business with the hospital and Dominick and..."

She stood still, knew she was glaring. He reached out and folded her into his arms. His hands were gentle as he raked his fingers through her hair, massaged her shoulders, and caressed her back. Finally, she started to think clearly.

"I know how hard all of this is has been for you," he said, "but if we're going to find the answers, we have to be rational."

"I *am* being rational, Harry. Who else would say something like, 'Don't get too comfortable?' It's exactly the kind of thing *he* would say. Besides, I know his handwriting."

"It's only a note, babe. It could be anyone trying to shake you up. Why are you so certain it's your ex? It's been years since you've seen his handwriting. If what you're saying is true, maybe he was the one who hijacked you in his truck?"

"It wasn't him."

"Then who? Just someone trying to shake you up?"

"Well, it's working. I mean. I just don't know anymore." Gina walked to the sofa and collapsed onto it. She covered her face.

Harry eased down next to her. "Come on, doll, it's going to be all right."

"Why can't people just leave me alone? I only want is to do my job and be with you."

"We both know nothing is that simple," he whispered in her ear.

She looked at him. "What do you mean?"

"This whole thing with Thelma doesn't surprise me."

"Again: what do you mean?"

"You've never been able to let things go, just let them ride. I think sometimes you care too much."

"Harry, how can a person care too much, especially in our profession?"

"Most of us wouldn't give a second thought to some of the things you pick up on. We put in our hours and go home. That's the end of it."

"Ha! No one is more dedicated than you, Harry Lucke."

"You are! It's never just a job for you, and never will be."

Gina smiled, then began to laugh. "Next thing I know, you'll pin a medal on me."

"I hope you know what a really big chance you took by turning in that culture when Taneka made it clear how she felt about the whole business."

"What Thelma is doing is horribly wrong. I honestly believe she's murdering these women. I can't just stand by and pretend it's not happening. And Taneka refuses to even consider that Thelma could be doing anything like that."

"But how sure are you? Really? Taneka could be right about the septicemia being just a lot of bad luck."

"Just because *I* couldn't pick up anything under the microscope doesn't mean the septicemia isn't originating from Thelma. It only means I don't have the right equipment to see what she's using to contaminate the KY jelly."

"True enough."

"Well, I should have an answer tomorrow," Gina said, "after they plate out the culture I sent in."

Gina grabbed onto his hand. "What do you really think, Harry?"

"Listen to me, beautiful: in the last three years I've seen your intuition at work. You have the nose of a bloodhound. If there's something out of whack, I believe you'll find it. But if you keep doing this kind of thing, one of these days somebody is going to chop off that pretty schnozzola of yours."

She gave him a fleeting smile. "I know it's Thelma. I know it ... just like I know Dominick left that note. I am *not* crazy"

"It doesn't matter. You don't want Taneka going to administration with ruffled feathers ... putting you back on the outs ... the same place you were three years ago."

"I guess."

"Then cool it."

"But—"

"—but look, listen, and keep thine lovely lips closed."

Chapter 46

Frannie Garrity was trying to make dinner while listening to one of Ryan's students butcher Beethoven's *Für Elise*; she wanted to yank out her hair.

When the twelve-year-old prodigy finally left, Ryan came into the kitchen and threw his arms around her. "I keep telling myself the kid will get better, but what do I know?"

Frannie held him at arms' length. "You know he will. All of your students do."

"Yeah, maybe." He moved to the coffee pot and splashed some into a cup that Frannie had created especially for him on her potter's wheel.

"I need to make you another coffee cup," she said. "That one is disintegrating before my eyes."

He laughed. "Yeah, sure. Do you know how many years it took to get you to throw this one?"

"I promise."

"When I have it right here in my hot little hand, then I'll believe it." He set the coffee down on the counter. "How did it go at the clinic today?"

"It was difficult, really difficult."

"I wanted to be with you," Ryan said. "You know that."

"Yes." She took his hand. "You were right, though ... we need the money from the new student. That piano lesson was more important."

"Being with you is important. I hated myself after you left."

"Let's just forget about it, even if it was pretty awful. I had the medical assistant from hell taking care of me."

"What happened?"

"I don't know. Nothing really. She made me feel dirty." She took a tentative sip of the coffee she'd just poured, made a face, dumped the rest out, and rinsed her cup in the sink. "How can you drink that sludge? Anyway, after tomorrow, it will all be over."

"Ironic. I just got the last sperm count test results back ... it was finally negative."

"Talk about closing the barn door after the horse is out."

"I've been thinking," he said, "if you really want to have the baby ... I'll go along with it. Maybe I can pick up some kind of day job."

"No, Ryan. We've gone over this from every angle and there's no way we can have another child. You are not giving up your music ... we both know that's what it would mean."

"But Frannie—"

She wrapped her arms around his waist and squeezed as hard as she could. "We'll do what we have to do." She whispered in his ear. "Besides, what would I do without your students' music to lighten up my day?"

* * *

The next morning, Frannie held onto Gina's hand as Dr. Forez placed the laminaria into her cervix. "I'm so glad you're with me," she said to Gina. "I don't think I could bear it if that other woman was here."

"I'm happy I can help." Gina said. "And you came through with flying colors."

"At this point, I just want to get the whole thing over with."

Dr. Forez removed all the instruments, peeled off her gloves, and held out a hand to help Frannie up. "I'll see you this afternoon."

"Thanks." She watched as the doctor washed her hands and then left the room.

"You do have someone to come pick you up this afternoon, don't you?" Gina said.

"Yes. My husband."

"Well, that's great ... because in the package of meds we gave you is a sedative. It's going to make you a little groggy ... or at least more relaxed," Gina said. "Can't let you behind a wheel that way." At the door, she smiled at Frannie. "See you later."

* * *

It had been difficult for Gina to concentrate on Frannie's procedure. Mostly, she was highly curious about were the results of the culture she'd sent into the lab for analysis.

Gina had made it her business to be the one doing the setup for Frannie. She wasn't about to let Thelma near the instrument trays, and as luck would have it, there was only one morning setup necessary – Frannie's.

Gina hurried back to the nurses' station, pulled up a chair, and scrolled through the lab test returns, looking for the results for the KY jelly culture. Her heart sank; nothing there. She went through the returns twice more.

Still not in. Damn!

When she turned away from the computer, Thelma was standing there looking over her shoulder.

Gina jumped. "For heaven's sake, Thelma, you scared me. Why did you sneak up on me like that?"

Thelma stepped aside, said nothing.

A jolt of fear raced up Gina's spine as she moved out of the station. When she turned around, Thelma was still looking at her with eyes that glowed with venom.

Chapter 47

Mulzini had been on the landline for at least an hour trying to get through to someone in the parole department of the New York correctional system. When he finally reached the right office, he was told, "We prefer to handle this kind of request by computer, with proper authorization by your Captain, or whoever is in charge there."

"That's not going to cut it," Mulzini said. "We're looking at a kidnapping and possible attempted murder here. We need that info now ... and if I don't get it, there's going to be hell to pay. Got that?"

"We have protocols, Inspector."

Well, good for you.

Mulzini was prepared to keep hassling this guy, and anyone else in New York, until he spoke directly to Dominick Colletti's parole officer.

"Are you still there?" he said.

"Hanging on."

He hoped against hope that Gina's brother was wrong about Colletti breaking parole, that all he'd heard was neighborhood gossip. It would make it so much easier if Gina's ex was in the Bronx, where he was supposed to be.

Mulzini had known Gina for three years and he still couldn't understand why anyone would threaten her, let alone want to kill her. It just didn't seem realistic. He wanted to prove that a mistake had been made and Gina's creepy ex was where he was supposed to be – in the in the Bronx being a good local hoodlum.

"Are you still there, Inspector?" said the nameless voice on the telephone.

"Yeah. I'm here."

"Sorry you had to wait so long. I finally pinned down Dominick Colletti's parole officer; I'll switch you over."

Mulzini wanted to make some smart-ass remark about the New York accent that he could cut with a knife, but he let it go and simply said, "Thanks."

"Yeah, Bashford here. What now?"

"Sorry to bother you Officer Bashford, but I'm Inspector Mulzini calling you from the San Francisco PD about one of your parolees."

"Yeah? That so?"

"Name's Colletti. Dominick Colletti."

"Yeah, what about him?"

Mulzini had had it. He was pissed. Dealing with New Yorkers had been nothing but a pain in the ass.

"What about him? I'll tell you what about him. He may have broken parole and is trying to kill his ex wife. Is that good enough for you, officer?"

"All right, already. Don't blow a gasket. You could have told me that right out of the gate, you know? Geesh!"

"Listen, man," Mulzini said, "I've been on this phone for more than hour trying to verify a simple fact. Has he broken parole or not?"

Mulzini could hear the guy's fingers tapping away at a computer keyboard.

"Afraid so. He's missed his check-in two weeks in a row."

* * *

Mulzini wished he were somewhere skipping rocks across the water. He needed that; it was the only thing that ever really calmed him down. Instead, he was steaming over the Colletti thing, wondering if the bastard really did cut Gina Mazzio's

233

brake line. Not only that, he was going to have to tell Gina that her ex was officially on the loose, whereabouts unknown.

He sat at his desk and looked around the office he shared with four other Inspectors. Right now, only Pepper Yee was there, with her ever-present piles of wandering papers covering her desk.

"Hey, Yee, when are you going to clean up that mess you call home? Probably a rat at the bottom, feeding off an old moldy hamburger you misplaced weeks ago."

She gave him her usual smart-ass retort, "Fuck you, Mulzini," and accompanied it with a digital salute. "The day you and Marcia take me to Hawaii instead of just running off and dumping your difficult cases in my lap, I'll have it spic and span for you."

He liked the Inspector – a lot. He was sorry to hear that she and her husband were calling it a day.

He seemed like a nice guy ... but what do I really know about anyone?

He turned away from her and continued his computer search for Katt's Apartment Management, the name Dirk thought he had seen on the door of the truck the guy had used to kidnap Gina, then dump her in Golden Gate Park. There were several Kats' with one t – none with a double t.

He thought he'd finally grabbed a break for Gina, but it was all ending up in a blind alley, with her ex hidden somewhere behind a trash bin.

She's going to go ballistic when she finds out Colletti's gone missing. Someone upstairs ought to give that nurse a break. Trouble always has a way of finding her.

Now, like it or not, Mulzini had to accept that it *could* have been her ex who cut the Fiat's brake line. Really not too hard to believe.

One thing Mulzini knew for sure: it didn't take much for someone to go off the deep end. The human mind was a dark and vengeful place. People held onto the smallest of slights and would do anything to even a score. Steal. Torture. Murder.

He looked back at the computer screen and the long list of apartment management providers. Maybe the kid got it wrong. After all, it was dark out when Dirk read the name of the maintenance company on the truck door.

He thought about Dirk.

Marcia had immediately fallen in love with the boy. Mulzini had to admit he liked Dirk, too, liked having him around. He and Marcia rarely saw either of their sons, who were busy with their own lives. It was nice to be appreciated for doing nothing more than providing a bed to sleep in and food to eat. Too many take simple things like that for granted.

Yeah, we all take too much for granted.

Mulzini went back online and went through the Property Management directory again. He decided to start at the beginning of the *K's* instead of picking up alphabetically at *Katt-*. When he came to *Karsh,* he stopped. Three listings.

Why is that name so familiar?

He sat back in his chair and brought his feet up onto his desk.

"Better watch it, Mulzini," Yee said with a laugh. "The big guy says no feet on the desk. Too unprofessional."

"This is what I have for the big guy." Mulzini provided his own version of disdain; a two handed birdie. Both he and Yee laughed.

Chapter 48

Amory Mason was lodged in his favorite chair, trying to catch up on his book reading. It wasn't going well. He'd been jumpy every since that nonsense with Marvin Karsh. He hoped it would all pass by without his having to get involved in it.

He'd recently started Dickens' *Great Expectations* and had been enjoying it ... until Karsh kidnapped that damn nurse.

He ran his hand across the book's leather binding and sighed. The information age, with all its technology, was something he had no trouble comprehending, but who had the time to keep up with it? Dickens's world, though, had greater depth, with real characters, people whose motives and actions were far more understandable.

He ran a finger behind the bookmark and opened to the page where he'd left off reading. Before he got half way through the first sentence, someone started pounding on his front door. He was startled, then angry, then up and out of his chair in an instant.

"For cryin' out loud! Ring the bell! That's what it's there for." He walked up to the door, flung it open. "What the hell is the matter with..."

His heart skipped a beat. The Karshes stood there, their faces a mixture of anger and determination. No one said anything for a long moment until Thelma finally broke the silence with a terse, nasty demand. "We need to talk, Amory. Now!

He wanted to slam the door shut, was disgusted with the pair of them. The mere sight of the Karshes made his stomach roil. These two specimens were the perfect example of the kind of people he'd always tried to avoid throughout his career – ignorant, pushy, crass.

Unfortunately, they were also the kind of people The Holy Eye seemed to attract.

Scrutinizing the couple, he realized they were not only aggressive, but homicidal – like too many within the group he'd started simply to keep himself busy following his retirement. He'd begun to think that pushing buttons – computer and telephone – was more in line with his style of protest. It was the smarter and safer thing to do.

Right now, Thelma and Marvin Karsh were convincing him that perhaps he should be thinking about how to back away and pass leadership of The Holy Eye on to someone else. Certainly not to these two cretins.

He could see that there was no way he was going to get out of letting them into the house without causing a ruckus. Just the look on Thelma Karsh's face told him that.

"Come in," Amory said, stepping aside. The couple proceeded him, walked into the living room, and, uninvited, sat down.

Amory ignored Thelma and her fiery eyes and spoke directly to Marvin. "What's the problem?"

Marvin said nothing. He seemed tongue-tied. He hadn't uttered a word since appearing at Amory's door.

"The nurse is still alive!" Thelma sat up straighter. "Not only that, she knows what I've been doing."

Amory held up a hand. "Stop right there! I don't want to hear anymore about this. I've never wanted to be involved in anything illegal – certainly not murder. I told you that the other day, Marvin, when you brought that woman to my doorstep."

"You what?" Marvin exploded. "You don't want to be involved? What the hell does that mean?"

Amory held up his hand again.

"Don't try to put me off again," Marvin said. "We thought The Eye was supposed to be all about preventing murder, murder of the unborn. You're involved in that, all right."

"That's different," Amory said.

Thelma's upper lip curled into sneer. "What you mean is, it's safer ... for you ... keeps your neck out of a noose."

"I started this organization with one objective: Stop legalized abortion." Amory pointed first at Marvin, then at Thelma. "You two are going in a completely different direction. In fact, for the good of the group, I'm going to have to ask you to withdraw from the organization."

"You—"

"—shut up, Marvin." Thelma pushed her face toward Amory. "*You* are not going to order us to do anything."

"Get out of my house," Amory yelled. "Get the hell out before I call the police!"

Thelma unfolded from her seat; she suddenly seemed much taller.

"Go ahead, you hypocrite, call the police. We'll tell them it was your idea to kill the nurse, and anyone else whose abortion views and actions go against the teaching of The Holy Eye."

Marvin jolted up and stood next to his wife. "Yeah, so keep your big mouth shut. Ya hear?"

* * *

Back in the truck, Marvin reached for the beer he'd left in the cup holder. Thelma grabbed it first and threw the can out the window.

"Hey, what the fuck you think you're doing?"

"Just drive!"

"I'm not taking orders from you, either. I'm the man of the house and don't you forget it."

"Oh, I'm not forgetting anything, Marvin, *dear*. I'm not forgetting that fat hand of yours beating up on me, your sleeping with every woman—"

"—I take care of you in the sack, don't I?" He swung his arm out and backhanded her in the mouth. "Don't you *poor Thelma* me, you bitch. When I hit you, it's because you deserve it." He twisted the key, started the truck, and pulled away from the curb.

Thelma pulled a wad of tissues from her purse, pressed them against her mouth, and caught most of the blood dripping down her chin. She eyed the roll of quarters he always kept in the glove box to feed parking meters, bit back the tears that threatened to gush. She was sure one of her teeth was loose, if not broken. Her face hurt, but she wasn't afraid of him anymore. Disgusted, she threw the tissues on the seat between them.

"We need to get that nurse, and we need to get her now,' Marvin said. "I think she saw my face."

"And how do you propose we do that?" Thelma said. "You messed up our one and probably only chance to get her out of the way."

"Just like anything that's broken ... fix it!"

There was a volcano inside of Thelma, building, growing hotter, rising. She was through with doing things just because he told her to do them.

"I told you before, Marvin, I'm not doing any of this anymore. It's all on you, now."

"What are you mouthin' off about?" He looked away from the avenue, glared at her until a loud continuous blare of a horn behind the truck brought his gaze back to the road. With a yank of the wheel, he turned into a small side street, stopped the truck, and turned to her. "Whadda you mean you're not doing it anymore?"

239

There was a weakness in her knees, but she continued. "I don't want to rot in prison, you hear me?" She grabbed the door handle, ready to jump out if necessary. "It wouldn't be that hard to prove what I'm doing is infecting and killing those women. Unless I stop now, that nurse is going to nail me."

"So what? They're murderers. That's what abortion does, it murders." He grabbed her by the hair and yanked her head around to face him. "You'll stop when I tell you to. Ya hear me?"

She looked at her husband, scrutinized his dirty clothes, unshaven face. Thelma had never hated anyone as she did her husband at that moment.

"And the men who get the women pregnant? Aren't they murderers, too?"

"What kind of bullshit is that? Men want to fuck ... that's it. The women are the murderers ... they're the ones who allow someone to have their holy creation destroyed."

"I don't care anymore. Do you hear me?" Thelma deliberately pulled his fingers from her hair, one at a time. She looked him square in the eye for a long moment – then she spit in his face.

He grabbed for the wad of tissues she'd thrown on the seat, swiped his face. His eyes were murderous; the muscles around his jaw were bunched. Thelma knew she should get out of the car and run. But it all seemed so unimportant now. She just plain didn't care. All she wanted was for him to kill her. Right here. Right now.

"You can do anything you want to me, Marvin. Even kill me. That way I won't get caught, won't have to die in prison."

"Fuckin' women! Think you can tell me what to do." He grabbed her arm; his fingers dug in.

Thelma snatched up the roll of quarters from the glove box, curled her fingers around it, and slammed him in the ear as hard as she could. "Did you think you could push me around forever, you lousy excuse for a man?"

His eyes filled with pain then morphed into the beady eyes of a cobra – cold, calculating.

Before he could speak, she said, "Get this through that thick head of yours, Marvin: either kill me here and now or start doing things my way."

Chapter 49

Gina shifted in bed, burrowed deeper under the covers while shadowy figures encircled her, closed in, pushed hard against her. One large hand, then another, reached out for her neck.

A loud voice screamed at her, *Maybe you'll stop bothering my wife now, bitch.*

She awakened with a start, her hands at her throat. Frightened and disoriented, she covered her mouth to stifle a scream.

The words continued to vibrate in her throat: *Maybe you'll stop bothering my wife now, bitch.*

She hadn't been thinking straight. Everything had happened too quickly – erratic, scattered. She'd only concentrated on Dominick and that had messed her up. It kept her from focusing on the bigger picture. Maybe her injuries had affected her more than she was willing to admit.

She started to reach for Harry, then changed her mind. He was exhausted from working overtime and he had the day off; he needed it, needed to get some rest, needed to sleep.

The alarm would go off in ten minutes so she decided to get up and start getting ready for work early now. She quietly slipped out of bed and turned the harsh alarm buzzer off before it could do its job and wake Harry. She walked into the living room, tried to make her thoughts come together.

When the results for the culture came in, she would have another talk with Taneka. Then there would be no denying what Thelma had done.

Gina wasn't sure how it was all going to tie together, but maybe Inspector Mulzini would be able to help her work it out. She planned to get in touch with him again as soon as she had the culture test results. She just knew they would be positive. They had to be!

Back in the bedroom, she tip-toed through the room, trying not to wake Harry, and went into the bathroom to brush her teeth and wash up. Gina looked into the mirror and studied her face.

What a mess.

She gingerly pressed her head, then her ribs and the other places where she'd been injured. She'd tried to ignore all of her painful symptoms from the car accident and kidnapping. But there was no getting around it: everything was still pretty tender.

She applied some drops to her reddened eyes and dabbed on some makeup, trying to lighten the dark circles under her eyes. The cuts on her arms from the automobile accident were looking good, well on the way to healing. When she took in the total picture, she saw herself covered with imaginary band aids – the only things holding her together.

You'll live!

She slipped into her scrubs, and stuffed her scissors, clamp, pen, into one pocket, her new cell in the other. She debated whether to kiss Harry goodbye or not, but chided herself – they'd always agreed that life was too tenuous, that each farewell could be their last.

She leaned over the bed, kissed Harry on the cheek. She hated to wake him since he didn't have to go in until the afternoon.

"Hey, doll," he mumbled. "Time to go already."

She looked into his blue eyes, which were at half mast. "Yes. You go back to sleep. I'll see you later."

Harry nuzzled her neck; his hands slid under her scrub top, then under her bra. He laughed. It sounded husky, sexy. "Come back to bed. I promise I'll be a quick."

"Some enticement."

She could tell from his voice that he was drifting off again, but he blew soft puffs of air into her ear. "How 'bout I meet you for lunch, doll?"

"Call me when you're fully awake."

His mouth was open as though he was about to say something, but instead he fell asleep again, snoring softly.

* * *

The Fiat barely gave her any trouble this time when she turned the key in the ignition – one little hiccup and that was it.

She gave it a pat on the dashboard. It was nice to have it back, the windshield and the bumper all repaired, and actually looking better than before the accident.

Even with all your idiosyncrasies, I love you ... and I know you love me.

At the hospital, she drove around looking for a parking place. The usual routine. She'd already given up the idea of parking in the garage. While circling the area, she reviewed what she would do after clocking in.

First thing, she would go to the computer and check for the lab results. She was certain Thelma had contaminated the KY jelly. So she knew in her heart that the lab results would prove her right. She could visualize the culture report on the computer screen – *Positive.*

Next, she would take the findings to Taneka and explain what Thelma had done, how she was responsible for Carrie and Elyse's deaths.

Gina was going to nail Thelma's hide to the wall.

With preparation for the condo construction underway, there was no curb space where she usually parked. She finally found an iffy spot about eight blocks from the hospital and refused to give in to her fears about the distance she would have to walk. She parked and took off at a rapid pace, pulled out her cell, and phoned Inspector Mulzini.

Might as well while I have the chance.

He picked up immediately. "I'm glad you called."

"Well, that's a first. I always imagine you rolling your eyes the second your phone window says it's me on the line."

"Not true at all."

"So what's up," Gina said.

"You first."

"I wanted you to know that I was able to get a sample of the contaminated jelly. I sent it to the lab."

"Are the results in?"

"I'm walking to the hospital now. I'll be there in a few minutes."

"Okay," Mulzini said. "So what's the last name of this medical assistant you think is causing the infections that are killing patients? You gave it to me once, but if I wrote it down, I've lost it."

"Her name is Thelma."

"Last name?" Gina could swear the Inspector was holding his breath.

"Karsh. Thelma Karsh. But listen, Inspector, there's more. I think it was her husband who kidnapped me."

"I'm beginning to think so, too. And, Gina, I want you to call me the minute those lab results are in, okay? We may have caught a break."

"What kind of break?"

"Later."

* * *

Gina hurried to the nurses' station, gave a big sigh of relief when she found it empty. She grabbed a chair and, with restless fingers, tapped into the lab results page.

Nothing yet? Dammit!

When she turned to leave, she came face to face with Thelma and Taneka.

"Thelma has made an excellent suggestion," Taneka said, smiling broadly at Gina. "She thought it might be a good idea if the three of us had lunch together and talked over some of the problems the two of you are having."

Thelma smiled at Gina. "I really think we can be friends. We just got off on the wrong foot."

Gina was stunned.

Never saw that coming.

Chapter 50

Harry called late in the morning, wanted to meet for lunch.

"You'll never believe it. Thelma, Taneka, and I are going to lunch ... together! Taneka is mediating ... thinks everything will be just dandy after we break bread together.

"Do you think it will work?"

"As far as I'm concerned, it's like going to lunch with Jack the Ripper."

"I guess there's no way out of it. Not if you want to keep your job."

"No, I'm trapped. Unless those lab results turn up first. And man, they better be positive."

"Be realistic, babe. The culture *could* be negative."

"Harry, I know Thelma is responsible for those women dying. And now I'm pretty sure it was her husband who tried to kill me. It all fits."

"You need hard facts, Gina."

"I know. No help from Mulzini without those requisite cold, hard facts."

* * *

Right up until they were out the door, Gina had hoped that the lab results would come in; it would have settled everything right there and then. But that wasn't happening.

For one last time before they left, Gina sneaked into one of the rooms to use the computer – the fourth time since she'd arrived for work that morning. She'd had to rush – it was only a few minutes before they were out the door for the high summit lunch. Keeping her fingers crossed didn't help her one bit. It was the same as the three previous times. No results.

"Why don't we go to the Bistro," Taneka suggested. "It's a nice little restaurant and the food is pretty good."

"That sounds like a great idea." Thelma said, smiling. "Their service is a little slow, but we've done it before without problems."

"Oh, we'll get back in time," Taneka said. "It's a good choice. Their booths make things more private."

Gina watched the two them confer as though she didn't exist.

Thelma finally addressed Gina. "We've eaten there before."

"So I hear," Gina said.

"It's only a mile from the hospital. but with the rain, walking is out."

"Works for me," Taneka said.

Did Taneka ever disagree with Thelma? This is creepy.

"Why don't I drive," Thelma said. "We can't fit into your car," she said to Gina, laughing. "Besides, we'd all be drowned before we could get to it."

Gina's pulse started racing.

There's only one way she could know anything about the car I drive. It was her husband who attacked me, then told her all about it.

In the elevator going down to the garage, Gina's claustrophobia was choking her. Thelma was close in on one side, Taneka on the other. It was like being at the bottom of a deep hole. She was desperate to escape. But there was no way out.

"It's a good thing I parked in the garage," Thelma said.

"We've had nothing but rain on and off for the past week." Taneka frowned. "Things are starting to flood."

Gina remained silent. She couldn't imagine why they were having this inane conversation when they were all probably going to spend an acrimonious lunchtime together.

* * *

By the time they ran into the restaurant from the parking lot, the three of them were pretty wet. At least the place wasn't too crowded –probably most customers decided it wasn't worth going out in the rain.

They were shown to one of the booths and given menus. Gina had no appetite, but she ordered roasted red pepper soup from a waiter who seemed to materialize right after they picked up their menus.

"Is that all you're eating?" Thelma said after ordering a meat ball sandwich.

"I always eat a light lunch." Gina's eye was starting to twitch a warning signal. Thelma had a self-satisfied look on her face, even with Taneka present. The medical assistant was usually more subservient around her.

"I always eat as if there's no tomorrow," Thelma said.

Taneka started to order her selection. "I think I'll have–" Her pager interrupted her. She held up a finger for the waiter as she punched in a number on her cell. She listened carefully before responding. "Oh, I'm not too far from the hospital. I'll catch a cab. Be there as soon as possible."

Taneka had a troubled grimace on her face. "Sorry. That was the administrator. They've set up an emergency meeting over another pending labor dispute. I can't get out of this."

Gina watched Thelma from the corner of her eye, but tried to keep her focus on Taneka.

"You two go ahead and have lunch," Taneka said. "You don't have to have me here. But please take notes so we can discuss it later. I'm confident you'll both work this out."

Gina blurted, "There's no point in our having a meeting without you, Taneka."

249

Taneka's face turned to stone. "Gina, if you want to keep this job, you will settle your differences with Thelma, right here and now. Am I clear?"

Gina nodded, but Taneka wasn't paying attention. She was already almost out the door to the restaurant.

Gina's neck was stiff and painful. "I want to go back right now, Thelma."

"If you say so, Gina. No sense just sitting here if you don't want to talk."

Caught off guard by the medical assistant's compliant response, Gina's thoughts were flying everywhere as they ran through the pelting rain to Thelma' car, leaving behind the restaurant and a disgruntled waiter.

* * *

Vinnie was in the hospital cafeteria during his lunch break; Helen sat directly across from him, a lovely smile on her face. She was speaking earnestly about something, but her voice was just a buzz of words to him. He didn't have a clue as to what she was talking about.

In the beginning, right from the moment they'd met, he'd not only felt happy and safe, but really on top of things, almost back to his normal, pre-war self. He was lulled into believing he didn't need Harry's or anyone else's help. All it was going to take was time and love. But during the past two nights, he'd reverted into the fearful, desperate man he'd become after his discharge, and before he'd met Helen.

He was having nightmares where he was alone and everyone around him was dead. Explosions and the cries of the wounded left him feeling torn and screaming.

Helen would wake him, hold him close until he dozed off into some kind of twilight sleep. One fact was clear: he hadn't really gotten better. In fact, he was worse since Dominick had come back into the picture.

He could not let that bastard hurt his sister. While no one else seemed to believe that Gina's ex was here in San Francisco, Vinnie did. He knew the man, knew what he was capable of doing.

"Vinnie!" Helen tugged at his hand until she pulled him out of his thoughts. "What's going on in that head of yours, big guy?"

"I'm worried about Gina."

"That's not what's causing your nightmares."

Vinnie held her hand. She was quite beautiful, with her huge eyes and soft mouth. All that sweetness and so much energy in such a tiny package.

"I guess it doesn't take much to make me feel threatened."

"Has Harry talked to his friend about you?"

"Good old Harry. I can see why Gina loves him so much."

"Lovely," Helen said. "But you haven't answered my question, dear boy."

"Next week. I have an appointment with a shrink that works with vets ... vets like me. You know, the damaged ones."

She smiled. "Don't you know, we're all damaged? No one gets away with a clean slate." She looked deep into his eyes. "At least we're going to get you some real help, Vinnie. And, darlin' boy, the sooner, the better."

"I can't stop worrying about my sister. Dominick could be here planning to kill her. I can't let that happen. Do you understand?" He squeezed her hand so tightly, she winced. "Oh, my God. I'm so sorry, Helen."

"Not to worry. Let's just make sure you get the help you need." She gave him a wide smile that made everything seem possible.

Chapter 51

The rain was coming down in sheets when they drove out of the restaurant parking lot. The deluge hammered Thelma's Honda, sounding like buckets of pebbles falling from the sky.

"Well, isn't this cozy?" Thelma said.

Gina said nothing. Without Taneka to neutralize the two of them, Thelma had dropped her cooperative façade.

"This is much better than sitting in a restaurant," Thelma said. "Why don't we just drive around for a while? We still have a few minutes before the lunch hour is over."

"No, I think we need to go back to the clinic. We can find an empty room and talk there."

Thelma let out a cackle that made Gina's heart freeze. "Why would I ever want to talk about anything with you?"

Gina shifted in her seat, looked back over her shoulder. "So, let's get back to Ridgewood. If we're not talking, I want out of this car."

"Want, want, want! Don't you think I have wants too? There're so many things *I* want. Instead, *I* get to enjoy your lousy company."

After that, Thelma went into silent mode but kept on driving rapidly through the heavy traffic even though visibility was severely limited. Some streets were now flooded, but Thelma managed to keep the car from getting stranded. It was miraculous that she didn't hit something, or that someone didn't run into them.

"Take me back, Thelma. Now!"

Thelma turned sharply onto an approach ramp to the Golden Gate Bridge.

Alarm cut through Gina. "Why are we crossing the bridge instead of going back to Ridgewood?"

"Because it's a beautiful bridge." Another of her heart-stopping cackles. "Because this is something *I* want. Is that good enough for you?"

"Look, Thelma, why don't we just cross the bridge, turn around, and go back to the clinic? We'll still have time to go someplace and work out our problems over a bowl of soup or something."

"Too bad you aren't one of those bitches looking for an abortion. I would have loved making sure you were sick as a dog ... sick like Carrie was."

Gina turned and glared at Thelma. "What?"

"Oh, yeah. She was just like you. Had no respect for me because I'm not an RN. Treated me like dirt ... just the way you do."

The wipers were loud, working hard without having any success in pushing the rain water away from the windshield. Gina could barely see through the glass; she was sure Thelma was having the same problem.

"I don't treat you like dirt, Thelma. I don't treat anyone that way—"

"—like I have no brains, can't do anything complicated or important, can't think on my own."

"I don't—"

"Oh, shut up! I'm so sick of you and your kind."

She flipped on the turn signal and cut off the freeway at the Sausalito exit. Even though it was slick from runoff flowing across the road like a river, Thelma continued to drive the twisty road at a constant speed – fast.

Gina wanted to grab the door handle and take her chances by flinging herself from the car. But even if she could get the seatbelt undone and open the door without Thelma stopping her, she'd probably break her neck rolling down a hill – especially at the speed they were going.

"Yeah, you're just like that Carrie. Fast talking, probably an easy lay ... probably just like the women Marvin's been fucking around with."

"Marvin?"

"Yeah, Marvin, my husband. You met the slob. He's the one who grabbed you off the street the other night. Thinks he's God's gift to women ... can do any damn thing he pleases.

They were driving through the center of Sausalito now. Gina's brain was working overtime.

Take the chance – release the belt, drop out of the car.

"If you have any ideas about getting out of my car, forget them." She held up a large syringe. "It's filled with Clorox. You touch the belt and this goes into your neck."

"Thelma, let's talk about this sensibly." Her mind was racing in all directions; she tried to slow herself down.

"There's nothing you can come up with that's going to make me like you or give a damn about anything you have to say." Thelma turned to look at Gina while the car careened down the street. The medical assistant laughed, obviously seeing the alarm on Gina's face before she turned her attention back to the road.

"Besides, you know what I've been doing and how I've been doing it."

"Why would you even want to kill those women?"

"That's a complicated question. One you probably think I'm too stupid to answer, but I'll try to make my little mind make it clear for you."

"I never said—"

"Women shouldn't be getting abortions. They were put on this good earth to have babies. And, as my husband would say, to be fucked. It's against nature, against God's will to have an abortion."

"So women shouldn't have any choice or control over their bodies?"

"No! We are God-given vessels, made to be filled ... not emptied."

"Is that the way you really feel?"

"Does it matter what I feel? My husband looked at me with respect for the first time when I came up with this plan to kill the sinners."

"If you don't believe in abortion ... don't have one. But you're committing murder, Thelma."

"An eye for an eye."

"Those women never did anything to you."

"An eye for an eye."

* * *

"Inspector Mulzini, please," Harry said to the officer who answered his call.

"He's kind of tied up. Who's calling?"

"Harry Lucke, a friend of his."

"Well, lemme see."

Harry thought about Gina while he was on hold. He had one of those weird feeling at the bottom of his stomach that Gina always described as a premonition. He didn't like the idea of Gina out with Thelma. The woman sounded pernicious and although Gina could never really identify Thelma's husband as the one who tried to kill her, the situation felt fraught with danger. The only redeeming feature was that Taneka was there, too.

"A friend, huh?" Mulzini said piping in on the telephone line."

Harry laughed. "What can I say? It's become our own private code. The people who man your phones guard you like an American treasure."

"And rightly so."

"Listen, Inspector, I'm worried about Gina."

"Harry, you ought to take that woman out and marry her once and for all. Marriage definitely dulls the senses and Gina could use a little of that."

"I'm not sure it would work in her case."

"Well, I spoke to her not too long ago. We're all waiting to see what that lab work shows. I'm betting that co-worker's husband is the one who nabbed her. A witness saw his home management sign on the door of the truck that carried her into the park."

"Isn't that enough to pick him up? I mean, you have a witness."

"It's not an exact ID," Mulzini said. "And Gina never saw his face. I need hard evidence to make anything stick."

"Yeah, well," Harry said, "I don't know. Maybe it's because I spend so much time with Gina, but her going to lunch with that Thelma Karsh makes me ... uneasy."

"Have you tried to reach her on her cell?"

"She's turned off. My calls keep going to her mailbox. That's just not Gina. It takes an act of God for her to turn off her phone." Harry laughed. "Unless she's pissed at me."

"We'll catch her at the hospital after lunch, Harry. Try and stay calm."

"I'll check back in with you in fifteen minutes or so."

"Good. You do that."

Chapter 52

Gina looked out at the rain-drenched streets, saw there were flood barriers up at several intersections. Thelma began to hum an eerie, off-tune song that made the hair on Gina's neck stand up.

After a long spell, the medical assistant said, "It was the first time I can remember Marvin bragging about me. We went to The Holy Eye meeting and he told everyone how smart I am. He'd never said that before."

"That's one of the anti-abortion groups, isn't it?" Gina said.

"Gee, aren't you the smart one."

"Do they know you've been murdering women?"

"They don't know the details." Thelma laughed. "I'm smarter than that. But they know I've been up to something ... something clever and good."

"It doesn't take too many brain cells to grow bacteria and hurt vulnerable women," Gina blurted.

The slap was sudden, hard, and stung.

"You smartass New Yorker. You probably grew up with a bank account and pretty clothes." Tears dotted Thelma's eyes. "Me, I've been waiting tables since I was sixteen ... lucky to finish high school."

"I learned to take care of myself the hard way, too, but I don't murder people because I don't agree with them. Do you know what a horrible death those women suffered because you deliberately filled them with bacteria?"

"Oh, shut up! I don't want to hear any more from you."

"Your thinking's really screwed—"

Thelma slapped Gina again. "Didn't I tell you to shut up?"

* * *

Taneka sat in the nurses' station, tap-tap-tapping her left foot. It was ten minutes past the time Thelma and Gina should have been back from lunch. The one remaining RN on the floor had called her out of her administrative meeting to help with the patient load.

The phone rang. It was Gina's fiancé, Harry Lucke.

"Ah, good," he said. "You're all back from lunch. May I speak to Gina, please?"

"She's not here," Taneka said. "She and Thelma haven't come back yet and I'm starting to get worried, what with all this rain and flooding."

"I thought you were having lunch with them."

"We went to the restaurant together, but I was called back for an emergency meeting of all the supervisors. They stayed on to have lunch."

"Well, like you say, maybe they're just dealing with the deluge," Harry said. "Traffic is probably a mess out there."

Taneka could tell he didn't believe it. "I'll have Gina call you as soon as she comes in."

"Okay, have her call my cell. I'm leaving here in a few minutes – grocery shopping, then home."

"Okay." She stood and paced back and forth. In addition to worrying about Thelma and Gina, she didn't like being called out of the administrative meeting to work the floor – it made her look weak, as though she couldn't run her department efficiently.

She sat down, scrolled into the computer, found Gina's new cell number, and called it. It rang and rang, finally went to the mailbox.

She also had Thelma's number on speed dial. It took only two rings for her to pick up.

"Yeah."

"Hi, Thelma, it's Taneka. Is there something wrong? The two of you are unreasonably late ... we're really jammed up here."

The phone went dead.

She hung up on me? What the hell's going on here. There better be a damn good explanation or heads are damn sure going to roll.

* * *

"That was Taneka, wasn't it?" Gina said. "Were you going to hijack her, too?"

"Yeah, I had plans for her, only *now* it's going to be easier with just you to deal with."

"But she'll be looking for us. And so will my fiancé."

"Give me your phone."

"No way."

"You listen to me ... you dig into that big bag you carry around and get that phone out."

"No!"

As swift as a viper, Thelma pulled the syringe from her pocket and held it up to Gina's neck.

"What, you think I won't use this?"

"All right." Gina put her hand in her purse and withdrew the cell, held it out to Thelma.

Thelma ignored her for a moment as she signaled and pulled off Sausalito's main street and onto the shoulder. "Okay, now toss the phone out the window."

"What?"

"You heard me. Get rid of it!"

Gina hit the button and the window rolled down, allowing a gust of wind and a funnel of rain to splash across her and the front seat. She threw the phone out and quickly brought the window back up.

Chapter 53

Harry stood at the apartment window, looking down onto the street. Rain was inundating everything, and he still hadn't heard from Gina. He watched water starting to back up from the street drains; it gave him a sense of foreboding He wanted to believe that Gina was all right, that the love of his life was safe, out of harm's way. But something told him she was in trouble; he was sure of that as he was of his own name.

He'd checked in again with Mulzini, who seemed to be moving at a snail's pace. He recognized that the inspector was a professional who wouldn't go off the deep end without evidence. But despite what Mulzini had told Gina, Harry didn't give a rat's ass right now about evidence – he wanted Gina back with him. Now!

Vinnie popped into his head, which also was troubling. Would Vinnie ever trust Harry again if he didn't tell him about what was going on with Gina? It would be much easier to dismiss him, say this situation was just another problem to add to his PTSD. But Harry knew better. Vinnie and Gina were not just close, they were extensions of one another. Vinnie would be furious if Harry withheld anything this serious, and rightfully so.

He turned away from the window and walked into the kitchen to put away the rest of the groceries he'd picked up from the supermarket on his way home. Shopping was a poor second to having lunch with the love of his life, but it was a diverting activity ... for a very short time.

He filled a glass with milk, right up to the brim. He sat on a counter stool and drank slowly. Since he was a kid, sitting and sipping milk allowed him to think and solve problems. Halfway through, he reached for his cell, which was charging on the kitchen counter.

He called Vinnie's hospital floor and asked to speak to him.

"Vinnie? It's me, Harry."

"What's up, man?"

"I'm worried about Gina."

Harry could hear Vinnie's breath catch before he answered. "Is it Dominick?"

"I don't think so. She went to lunch with that medical assistant, Thelma—"

"I know about that one. Gina told me she thought Thelma was responsible for the deaths of the abortion patients."

"That's the one."

"Why's she going to lunch with her?"

"It was supposed to be the two of them, along with the charge nurse, Taneka."

"And no one knows what's happened to them?"

"Taneka's had to go back to the clinic early and she has no idea what has happened to Gina and Thelma. The thing is, I didn't want you to be in the dark about it, Vinnie."

"You're home, right? I'll be right there."

"No Vinnie, wait!"

He'd hung up.

* * *

Vinnie's head was exploding. He went into the nearest bathroom, locked himself in a stall, sat down on the toilet, and covered his ears. The blasting noise, the resounding blasts wouldn't stop.

Boom! Boom! Boom!

"Can't do this," he said to the door. "Can't fall apart now. I can't. I can't. I can't." He closed his eyes.

Gina needs me ... needs me.

He began to rock back and forth. Rocking, rocking – it was the only thing that seemed to calm him. He filled his lungs with deep breaths, concentrated on the air that went in and out of his body. The noises started to subside, little by little.

He opened his eyes. He couldn't, wouldn't stay here.

* * *

"Inspector Mulzini, it's Harry again. Thelma and Gina still haven't returned from lunch." His voice caught in his throat. "Did you hear me? I tried to call Gina and her charge nurse said they never came back from lunch and no one has heard a word from them."

"And you said she was with Thelma Karsh?"

"Yes! *That* one!"

"Calm down, Harry. It could be nothing more than the bad weather ... flooding, a minor fender-bender, any number of things."

"I don't think you believe that any more than I do, Inspector. I want to, but I just can't. Gina's cell is turned off and Thelma answered a call from Ridgewood then immediately hung up. I know my Gina. She's in trouble. She needs us."

"Okay. Where are you?"

"I'm at home. My brother-in-law will be here any minute now."

"Is that the ex-Marine, the one who's working at Ridgewood?"

"Yeah."

"You two stay put ... you hear me, Harry?"

"Maybe you can GPS her phone. That might help."

"Okay, Harry. Good suggestion. Hang tight."

Chapter 54

Thelma parked her car in front of a dilapidated shed near the bay in northern Sausalito. "Did you think you could get away with pinning those deaths on me?" Thelma asked. "You may be a nurse, but you're not as smart as you think you are. Taneka would never believe you."

"How do you know what Taneka would or wouldn't believe?"

"That's a stupid question."

"Maybe I do underrate you, Thelma, but you sure as hell overrate yourself."

Thelma back handed her across the cheek again, fast and hard. Gina's head snapped from the jolting blow.

"Right here ... right now ... today, you're going to learn what it feels like to be powerless. Then you'll understand what my life's been like."

Gina bit back a retort. Thelma jerked the wheel to the right and turned off the main road. They drove toward the bay, then turned into a short flooded alley that fronted a row of gray, shed-like buildings. A white, crewcab pickup was parked in front of the sheds, its tires in about a half a foot of water.

Gina looked long and hard at the truck. Her heart lurched; she wasn't certain it was the same vehicle she had been thrown into a few days ago, but it sure as hell looked familiar. A man was sitting behind the wheel; he opened the door, jumped down, and sloshed through the accumulated ground water toward the passenger side of the Honda.

"Get out!" Thelma ordered.

"Can't you and I settle this?"

Thelma had a broad smile on her face. "I believe this is when snotty people like you want to overlook our differences and just go along with the program."

"Please, Thelma."

"There's nothing to settle, Miss High 'n' Mighty. We're never going to come to an understanding. And with you gone, I can continue to punish those murdering women. It might be at a different hospital or clinic, but I know how to do it now. I can go anywhere." Thelma laughed. "Maybe I'll even get a job at Planned Parenthood."

"You're day-dreaming, Thelma. People know about my suspicions. I've spoken to the police department, my fiancé, Taneka." Gina could hear the desperation clinging to her words. "I sent a culture to the lab of that bacteria-filled jelly you've been using to cause septicemia."

Thelma gave her that horrible cackle again, only this time it went on and on. "Did you hand-deliver that culture to the lab, Nurse Mazzio?"

Gina's breath caught in her throat. She knew what was coming. She'd made a fatal mistake by putting the culture into the delivery cart for pickup instead of taking it to the lab herself.

"Well, did you?"

Gina was silent.

"They'll get a culture all right, but it will be one of nice fresh KY jelly. Not a microbe in sight." She jabbed a finger into Gina's arm. "I told you not to underestimate me."

Gina turned away from Thelma's ruthless gaze.

"Now, get out!"

"How are you going to explain my disappearance, Thelma? Everyone knew we were going to lunch together. They'll come after you."

"Marvin and I will be long gone by the time they find you. And trust me, you won't be in any shape to say anything."

"Thelma!"

"Get your ass out of the car. Now!"

* * *

Vinnie and Harry waited for Mulzini in the apartment. Vinnie had just walked away from his job without a word to anyone.

"You shouldn't have done that, Vinnie. You really should have stayed have stayed until they brought on a replacement. You'll probably get fired for this."

"Fuck it! I couldn't care less about that right now," Vinnie said. "This is about Gina. She's in trouble." He gulped down a glass of water. "Why wouldn't anyone listen to me, to her, when she said Dominick was here and was after her? Even after the cut brake line, no one would listen."

"Hey, man, this is not Dominick! How many times do I have to tell you that."

"I don't believe it. It's him! He's in San Francisco and he's after her."

"Vinnie, sit down in one place and listen."

It took Vinnie a moment, but then he dropped down into the sofa and let his legs sprawl out in front of him.

"Gina went out to lunch with Thelma Karsh and they never came back. Thelma's married to Marvin Karsh and Mulzini thinks he's the one who kidnapped Gina, tried to kill her, and then bury her in Golden Gate Park." Harry eased down next to his future brother-in-law. "It's not Dominick!"

"I know that bastard is in the mix somewhere."

There was a knock at the door. Harry and Vinnie jumped up like twin puppets. When Harry went to the door, it was Mulzini.

"Hi, didn't hear you ring the entry buzzer," Harry said.

"I came in the building with one of your neighbors." He looked at Vinnie and said, "You even look like your sister." The

Inspector shook Vinnie's hand. "Thanks for keeping us safe over there."

Vinnie flushed as he always did when anyone mentioned his service in the military. "What do you plan on doing, Inspector? Where are we going?"

"The two of you can ride along this time, even though I don't like it one bit. But I can't have you both out of control, doing something stupid, and messing up everything. That's the only reason I agreed to take you along. At least I can keep an eye on you."

"Never realized you had such a low opinion of me," Harry said.

"Come on, Harry. It's your gal out there. Can't expect you to be at the top of your game with this whole business still hanging. By the way, was there ever a result on that culture Gina was talking about?"

"Yeah, I called in," Harry said.

"Well?"

"No apparent growth. It was negative."

"Well, shit, that really complicates things," Mulzini said. "That was going to be my hard evidence."

Vinnie started pacing. "Okay, okay. Let's stop the talk and start doing something."

* * *

"There's the number! That's the apartment complex," Harry said as they drove up to where the Karshes were listed as living.

"Okay. Harry, Vinnie, you stay in the car."

"We want to go with you," Harry said.

"Well, Harry, that's just tough shit. The both of you are going to stay right here, and if you give me any lip you're going to be taking a cab back to your apartment, unless you prefer to

267

walk." He got out of the car and leaned in through the open door. "Don't make me any sorrier than I am right now that I brought the two of you with me."

Both of them shut up and nodded.

Must be getting soft in my old age bringing two civilians along with me.

The complex was one of those mid-priced affairs that probably nabbed way too much money for just the average Joe to live in.

But looking at the lineup of buzzers, he could see the place was probably full up. There was a name next to each slot.

He buzzed the Apartment Manager and waited.

Nothing.

He poked *#101* on the first floor. Almost immediately he was buzzed in.

A tall woman, not much older than Mulzini and with large inquisitive eyes, opened the door and stepped into the hallway.

"May I help you?"

He pulled out his badge and ID; she looked at them very carefully. He knew she was memorizing all the pertinent info.

"I'm looking for the manager."

"He's not here. I saw him drive away in his truck a while ago."

"What kind of truck does he drive?"

"No idea. Just a white pickup as far as I'm concerned."

"A crewcab?"

"Don't know what that means."

Mulzini sighed. "Extra space behind the seats for more people to ride."

"Oh, yeah. I think that's what he drives."

"I see. Is there anything you can tell me about him?"

"Has he done something wrong?"

Mulzini used a small shrug as an answer.

"He's okay. He'd have more time to do his job if he'd stop trying to mess around with all the female tenants."

"Has he tried to hit on you?"

Her face lit up and she gave him a wide smile. "He's not that dumb. He knows I keep a baseball bat behind the door for just that occasion."

Mulzini laughed. "If you have an emergency relating to the apartment and he's not here, how do you get in touch with him?"

"I have his cell number. Let me get it for you."

Chapter 55

Gina stepped out of Thelma's car into ankle-deep water. She looked at the tall, thin man who was carrying a large backpack over one shoulder. A sudden downpour of rain, driven by a strong gust of wind, drenched every inch of her.

As he got closer, she could smell him. One whiff, even diluted by the heavy moisture, told her he was the same man who had grabbed her and thrown her into his truck.

You asshole! Tried to kill me! Bury me!

"I had you the other day, didn't I?" the man said. "Thought you and I had finished our business ... thought we were done with each other." He gave a nasty grunt. "My momma always said," – he took a moment to cross himself – "never leave a job unfinished. And Marvin always made momma happy."

Gina was speechless. All she could think about was running, running as fast and far away as possible ... run like she always had to as a little girl. Get away! Get away now! They were going to hurt her, kill her.

Run!

It must have been plastered all over her face because Marvin clamped a hand onto her arm; she wasn't going anywhere.

Thelma came and took hold of her other arm. "In the time I've known you, Gina Mazzio, you can't seem to ever button that lip of yours. Now you have nothing to say? Nothing?"

Marvin pulled a ring of keys from his belt loop and went through several before finding the right one to open the padlock on the shed's door latch. The door almost fell off its hinges as he pushed it open. The whole barn-like structure looked like it might collapse at any moment.

When Thelma tried to push her forward, Gina dug her heels into the mud. Heart thrumming, she tried to scream, but Marvin smothered her mouth with one hand and yanked her inside.

Her eyes adjusted almost instantly. It was dim but she could see the interior was probably made up of at least two small rooms; chunks of muddy wood were floating on a flooded dirt floor. It was empty – there wasn't a stick of anything in the building, and it was cold as an icebox. She was covered in goose bumps; her breath flew out and misted around her.

"Cozy little place," Thelma said, and punctuated her words with her infuriating cackle.

Marvin laughed, too, as though Thelma had said something really clever. "The owners used to rent this mess to artists, like real cheap ... no one else wanted to stay and work in this shithole, much less pay rent. When the land was bought up, no one wanted the fucking sheds for anything – and everyone was kicked out. This mess is coming down in a few weeks for redevelopment."

Gina twisted her face away from Marvin's hand. "Let me go," she yelled. "I won't tell anyone about this."

"Do you believe her, Thelma?"

"Not in a heartbeat."

"See there? If Thelma don't believe you, how can I." He bellowed out another laugh that made Gina's ears hurt; he dragged her farther inside.

The room once had a large window that now showed nothing but spikes of glass sticking out of the frame; the roof was caved in at one corner, allowing the rain to blow into the room. Water also flowed freely in and around the bottom of the rotted and splintered wood siding.

Without warning, Marvin flung Gina to the floor. She was instantly covered in filthy, sucking mud. He gave Thelma the backpack to hold while he unzipped the top. Unraveling strands of clothesline popped out over the upper edge of the bag.

Marvin pulled out a few lengths, then a few more and then shook his head angrily. "Shit!" he shouted. "Planned on hog-tying the bitch, but I cut the rope too damn short."

Gina knew her eyes were wide with terror as he grabbed her arms and tied them behind her. She was sloshing around in the muddy water, trying to get a hold on something solid, trying to get away from him. He roughly rolled her onto her stomach; her face went down and was buried in the muck. She tried to scream, but couldn't breathe past the ooze.

He grabbed her by the neck and yanked her up.

"Oh, no! You don't get off that easy, nursie. You're gonna die in this room all right, but you're gonna see it coming as you lie here and rot." He grabbed her ankles, tied them together, and dragged her closer to the outer wall. He used a finger to swipe the mud away from her nose and mouth. "I feel kinda mean spirited about you, since you were supposed to be finished business, only it turns out not to be so finished after all." He smiled at her. "Know what I mean?"

Thelma, listening to him, was hysterical, laughing so hard she bent over and clutched her middle.

Suddenly, Marvin grabbed his wife by the neck, yanked her close, and punched her in the face over and over until one roundhouse right broke her nose. Blood flowed like a river.

"What are you doing," Thelma cried out, her words bubbling through the blood. "We were going ... going to run away together. What—"

"Run away with you?"

"Yes!"

"You're old, Thelma. Your boobs are ugly ... and you can't give me a son, the son you were supposed to give me years ago. I want a son! You hear me? I want a son!"

Thelma could barely croak out one word, "Who?"

He ignored her while he took more rope from the backpack, tied two long lengths together, and hogtied her, wrists to ankles.

"Who?"

"Oh, yeah, who? You've seen her, Thelma ... it's that pretty little filly in number two-o-three. Oh, man, we've been going at it for months. And would you believe it? She's pregnant. With a boy. A goddam son!"

"Marvin, please don't. We had our babies ... we've had a life together."

"Yes, bitch, *had* is the word. *Had!*"

His face turned flint hard as he flipped Thelma onto her stomach. "Hey, Thelma, I'm gonna leave it up to you. – you'll last as long as you can keep your face out of the water and mud."

Gina curled into a ball. Tried to make herself smaller and smaller.

Chapter 56

"They're still not back," Harry said after breaking his cell connection with Taneka.

"And they've been out of touch now for what, nearly four hours?" Vinnie said. "What the hell's going on?"

Mulzini was still ignoring Vinnie and Harry, who were sitting in the back of the plain-Jane police sedan outside Gina and Harry's apartment. He hadn't spoken a word to them since he started tapping away at the keyboard of his dashboard computer.

"Inspector, why are we just sitting here?" Harry said.

"We'll never find Gina this way," Vinnie chimed in, his voice coming out very loud in the closed vehicle.

The Inspector kept at his typing. "Hmpf!" he grunted and turned back to face them.

"I Got a GPS location for Gina's cell. We're headed for Sausalito."

"Anything on Karsh's truck?" Harry asked.

"Not yet."

"What do you think that means?"

"Haven't the slightest."

"This is bad. Really bad ... I know it," Vinnie said to Harry.

Harry wanted to reassure him but couldn't. Fear was clenching his gut and he knew if he spoke he would heave all over the back seat.

"Knock off the friggin' whining! I mean, cut it out right now!" Mulzini turned back to the front, slapped the steering wheel. "Damn! No good deed ever goes unpunished."

Harry and Vinnie stared at Mulzini's scowl in the rear view mirror.

"I swear, I'll throw you both off the Golden Gate Bridge if you keep talking that gloom and doom crap." He slapped the seat beside him. "Another example why we don't like ride-along civilians."

"I'm sorry, Inspector," Harry said. "We're more than just a little worried here."

"Well, hell, Harry," Mulzini's voice getting louder to match Harry and Vinnie's. "I'm worried, too. I've come to like that little scamp from the Bronx." He looked at Harry in the mirror. "We'll get Gina ... ya hear me? We'll get her!"

Yeah, Inspector, I know you will. But will she still be in one piece?

* * *

"According to our IT, this is the spot where Gina's phone should be," Mulzini said.

The Inspector pulled off to the side of Bridgeway. The three of them got out of the car.

"It's got to be right around here, probably on the ground somewhere since there aren't any trash cans in sight." He started walking in ever-increasing circles, his eyes always looking down. Now and then he would kick at a candy wrapper, soda can, or other piece of trash.

Harry and Vinnie started doing the same thing.

"Criminals are pretty damn smart today," Mulzini mumbled. "It's a wonder we pick up anyone." He shook his head. "Technology, technology." He looked through the weeds and under scraggly bushes. "Whoever has her, probably ditched her cell so we couldn't find her."

Harry walked a little farther away, toed something, then picked it up. "Found it!" He brushed the dirt off a battered smart phone. "It's Gina's, her new one," he yelped. "I'd know it anywhere by the case." Vinnie moved in next to him and took the cell from his hand.

The Inspector smiled at them for the first time. "Maybe the two of you are good for something after all."

Chapter 57

Marvin's boots were ankle deep in mud and the water was rising fast. It came down like a waterfall from the caved-in roof. The glassless window, and disintegrating wood beneath it, contributed their part by allowing the cold rain to blow in through the opening and flow under the rotted siding.

"Well now, ladies, it's time for me to trot along. Me and my sweetie and our little baby boy plan on traveling down the road a piece. Maybe San Diego. Nice and warm *and*," he laughed, "*dry*."

He moved up to the vertical slats under the window frame – one kick was all it took for a couple of pieces of wood to drop. With less obstruction, runoff from the back side of the building streamed in faster.

He looked at Gina for several seconds; she guessed he was making sure the ropes around her wrists and ankles were still holding. Then he toe-nudged Thelma's shoulder, which was now half buried in the watery muck. It looked like he was going to say something to her, but instead, he turned and sloshed through the mud and on out through the door.

"Marv..." Thelma tried to call out. "Ma..." But the words were garbled; Gina could barely make them out.

He never looked back.

* * *]

"Based on the cellular info we got from Karsh's tenant," Mulzini said, "I now have his truck license number and a positive GPS fix on his location. He's about three blocks from us, traveling in the opposite direction, back toward the bridge."

277

Harry wanted to say *something, anything,* but his throat was too dry, he couldn't utter a word. He turned to Vinnie and saw him sitting on the edge of the seat, his neck tensed like a coiled spring.

Mulzini clamped his portable, flashing red light onto the roof of the sedan and flipped the switch for the siren as they hit the main thoroughfare. Traffic started pulling over, getting out of their way. He made a screeching turn that took them through downtown Sausalito and to the bypass road leading to the Golden Gate Bridge.

"There's our fine, upstanding Mr. Karsh ahead of us," Mulzini called out. "He's about to drive onto the bridge."

Harry could see the white pickup about a half-dozen car-lengths in front of them.

Mulzini used his radio to request assistance from any nearby cruisers, the bridge police, and the California Highway Patrol.

Harry didn't catch all of it but he did hear the words "kidnapper" and "possibly armed and dangerous." It left no doubt that Mulzini fully intended to catch Karsh.

When they got close enough to the pickup to see inside, Harry's breath caught — only the driver was visible.

"Where the hell's Gina?" Vinnie moaned.

The Inspector held up a hand. "Hold on. Let's wait and see what's in the crew cab, or the bed of the truck."

Marvin made no attempt to pull over, even though they were close enough for him to see the red lights reflecting in the truck's rearview mirrors.

Bridge drivers were honking horns and rubber-necking as Mulzini worked his way up alongside the truck, flipped on his microphone, and shouted, "Pull over, Mr. Karsh ... you're not going anywhere."

The truck kept moving.

"Ram the bastard," Vinnie yelled.

"Not in the middle of the bridge," Mulzini said, then held the microphone to his mouth again.

"Karsh! Pull over! Now!"

Marvin finally veered over to the far right, slowed to a halt.

Mulzini cut in front of the pickup and stopped just as a Sausalito police cruiser, its rack of lights flashing, blocked the truck from the rear. Before anyone could open a door, two CHP cars were on the scene also.

Mulzini and two other officers jumped out of their vehicles into the heavy rain and positioned themselves behind car doors, weapons at the ready. Mulzini, pistol held out in front of him with two hands, approached the driver's door of the truck.

Karsh was sitting inside, both hands on the steering wheel in the three and nine o'clock positions. Mulzini motioned for him to roll down the window, then rose up on his toes to peer inside the back of the crewcab. He couldn't see all the way to the floorboards, but it was obvious there was no one inside the cab except Karsh. He looked to where Harry and Vinnie sat waiting and shook his head negatively.

"Where's Gina Mazzio?" he asked through the now open window.

Karsh's unblinking eyes looked straight at Mulzini. "I don't know what you're talking about, sir. And just who is Gina Mazzio?" He rested an elbow on the window ledge and pushed out a hand. He watched the rain wash away the accumulated dirt on his palm. "Horrible weather we're having."

One of the CHP officers opened the passenger-side door. "Open up the glove box, sir."

Marvin took his time, making great pantomime of stretching across the cab to open the box. The officer directed his flash inside the small compartment.

"Nothing here," he said. Then he crawled into the crew cab and pulled out a Remington .30-06 carbine from under a blanket. The four–round magazine was fully loaded.

"You're right, Mr. Karsh – weather's certainly too horrible today for game-hunting," Mulzini said.

Marvin looked away from the Inspector. "Never know when you might see a coyote. More and more of them around these parts lately."

"Where's your wife, Thelma?" Mulzini demanded. "Has she taken Gina Mazzio someplace?"

Karsh shrugged.

That slight movement set Mulzini off. "You piece of shit!" He grabbed Karsh by his extended arm and pulled him part way out the door window. "We know from the GPS in Mazzio's cell that you probably stashed her someplace in Sausalito."

Marvin neither moved nor changed expressions.

"We also know that your wife went to lunch with Ms. Mazzio, and that neither of them returned to work. My guess is that if we find your wife, we'll find Gina Mazzio as well."

"I don't know what you're talking about. I can't help you when I don't know squat ... Inspector."

"I doubt that. And whatever *is* going down here, we're pretty damn sure you're in on it."

"In on what? I just took a little trip to Sausalito. Is that a crime?" He shrugged his shoulders again. "I'm an American citizen, Inspector, and I can go anywhere I damn well please. This isn't a police state ... at least not yet."

"Right now, you're suspected of aiding and abetting the kidnapping of Gina Mazzio. You could save yourself a lot of grief by simply cooperating."

"Kinda hard to offer any help when I don't know what you're talking about."

Mulzini turned and asked one of the CHP officers if he'd be willing to haul Karsh to a holding cell. The patrolman checked with his dispatcher, said it was okay. They loaded Marvin into the CHP cruiser.

"We'll go back to where we picked up that signal from his GPS and see what we can find," Mulzini said.

"How well do you know the town?" the Sausalito officer asked.

"Not much better than the average tourist, I suppose." He indicated the backseat with a nod of his head and added, "And I'm not expecting too much help from these two."

"I'll follow along behind and when you get to the location, I'll do what I can to help you."

"Great."

As they pulled away, the bridge police were directing a tow truck to haul Karsh's pickup, and the CHP was getting traffic moving again.

Chapter 58

"Lift your head, Thelma!" Gina shouted. "You've got to keep your face out of the water!"

Using her butt and the heels of her bound feet, Gina scooted and slithered backwards through the muck toward Thelma, not sure if the woman was even conscious.

Almost there, her heels lost their grip, sending her backwards with a violent lurch. Bolts of pain shot up into her neck. She screamed, the sound bouncing off the dilapidated walls. She twisted her torso, tried to relieve the tension in her arms before she dislocated one or both of her shoulders. She tumbled over to land face-first in the flood water and mud. She fought to lift her head, but it wouldn't budge.

No air got through. Her lungs screamed to exhale and pull in more oxygen. She strained, tried to rock her body, pushed in every direction. She remained stuck in that position. When the last of her air exploded with a sickening burble, she made one more effort. There was a loud sucking sound and her head broke free.

Her heart pounded violently as she snorted and coughed out the mud jammed in her mouth and throat.

Thelma!

Not a sign of movement. She was either still unconscious, or had given up.

Gina squirmed up against her, used her forehead to nudge Thelma's head up high enough to see her face. What looked back was an apparition of coal-black eyes, an exposed crusted tongue, and a drooping mouth. Her hair was an eerie mass of coiled Medusa-like strands.

"Thelma?"

"Go wa."

"Let me try to help you."

Thelma gurgled an "Oo" and drove her face back into the muddy water.

Gina shivered and her teeth chattered. Both she and Thelma were now deeper in the still-rising flood of rain water.

Need to stand.

She looked again at Thelma and knew that if she lost her footing, she would be finished also.

She tried for the third time to force her tightly-bound hands into the pocket where she carried her bandage scissors. She pushed and pushed until her arms and hips were set in a near-dislocating position. Then her fingertips caught the slim edge of material, which she gathered bit by bit until she was far enough into the pocket to grab one loop of the scissors. She pulled slowly, slowly until it almost lifted out. It slipped away and fell back into the drenched, mud-slick pocket.

Her shoulders shook; her sobs filled the cavernous room.

Harry! Where are you? I'm so cold ... cold.

Thelma knew how this would end. Made it all happen on her terms.

Cold, tired.

Gina's eyelids sank shut.

Her mind drifted. Sleep was closing in, along with a deep chill that left her breathless.

Rainbows. Splotches of blue, yellow, purple, and orange surrounded her.

"Have to stop breaking the glass, Vinnie," she mumbled. "You break the glass, you kill the beautiful rainbow."

Silly kid. Loved rainbows. Never figured it out. Just a small lie for my ornery little brother. Only way to keep him from breaking the neighbors' windows just for the hell of it. Silly, silly, silly.

A loud bang jolted her. Her eyes popped open. The caved-in roof at the corner of the shed had collapsed, fell within a couple of feet of her.

I'm going to die here. Die here without ever seeing Harry again.

So sleepy.

Her eyes closed.

Beautiful rainbows. Vinnie, remember the beautiful rainbows?

A germ of a thought got through the exhaustion. Her eyes snapped open.

Rainbows! Broken glass! The window!

It was such a long way to go. She couldn't feel her arms, and her legs didn't want to respond as she scrabbled toward the window. The rain was still blowing in, tap-tap-tapping against her mud-caked face. She could barely move her cheeks, open her mouth. Gust-blown water hit her tongue, slipped down her throat.

The frigid water made her fingers wooden as she dragged them through the mud; she nudged a triangular piece of what she hoped was glass. Her fingers were too numb to be sure.

The water had soaked the rope Marvin used to bind her hands and feet. She used the edge of the shard to saw at the fibers.

Slow. Too slow.

She needed to get free, to stand.

The slippery floor made it difficult to get her legs under her. She braced her back against the rickety wall beneath the window frame, contracted and released the muscles of her back and butt.

She began to move upward ... slowly.

The wooden siding gave way and she fell out of the shed.

Chapter 59

Gina's eyes fluttered open, stared into the deluge of rain. It was like someone was pouring buckets of water on her from high up in the sky.

She was confused. The last thing she remembered was falling through a wall, hearing the sound of splintering wood.

Now she was outside. She wanted to yell for help but her throat was constricted ... no sound escaped her lips.

Exhaustion kept her down and she began to drift off, drift away.

Sleep. Need to Sleep.

Sharp, stabbing pain in her arms awoke her.

She turned her head, slowly, painfully. She was outside a ramshackle shed, a short distance from the bay.

She stared at the shed. There. I was in there.

She watched the pounding rain sweep into the building. The place where she'd been taken, tied up, left to die.

Thelma! Marvin!

Thoughts, images flashed through her head, coming at her as fast and as heavy as the rain.

She looked into the shed for Thelma. But all that was left of her was an island surrounded by muddy water.

Gina cried. Her body shook from intermittent spasms. Pins and needles stabbed her fingers.

Need to get up.

It took three excruciating tries just to get onto her knees. Chin down, she stared at several pieces of broken window glass beneath the shattered window.

She picked up a jagged piece and began again to saw at the wet rope that bound her hands behind her. Twice she lost her finger-grip on the shard and cut herself. The rain-blood

Bette Golden Lamb & J. J. Lamb

combination made the sharp glass even more slippery, but eventually, through the pain, she felt one strand after another separate. Slowly, ever so slowly, the rope loosened enough for her to free her hands.

* * *

Mulzini pulled up and parked along the edge of Bridgeway at the spot where they'd found Gina's cell earlier. The Sausalito cruiser stopped also.

"I say we head north," Mulzini said. "We'll hit every street in a five to ten-block radius."

Harry's stomach churned until he thought he was going to retch. How were they ever going to find Gina? Mulzini's suggestion seemed like such a long shot.

They've killed her. She's dead. That's why Karsh wouldn't say anything.

Harry looked into Vinnie's eyes, saw shock. The heels of Vinnie's hands squeezed his head at the temples; low guttural moans filled the back of the police car. Harry threw an arm around Vinnie, pulled him close. "Come on, man, it's going to be okay. It has to be."

But Harry knew it wasn't.

"Listen, you two," Mulzini said, "don't give up on me now." He signaled and pulled back out onto Bridgeway, the Sausalito cruiser, lights flashing, close behind.

Harry wanted cry out. He couldn't stand the thought of losing Gina, but he had to hold himself together, not only for himself, but for Vinnie. If the ex-marine lost it or freaked out, they might never bring him back out of it.

"Any suggestions which way we should go?" Mulzini asked the Sausalito cop over the radio.

"Doubt if there's much chance of finding her in any of the occupied commercial buildings here along Bridgeway," the officer said.

"What's farther down the street?"

"Pretty much the same until Bridgeway merges with the freeway headed north. My suggestion would be to go off to the right toward the water. There are a lot of old sheds, small warehouses, and that sort of thing out there."

"Works for me," Mulzini said.

The cruiser pulled ahead and turned into the first side street that went toward the waterfront. They followed him through the mixed-use industrial area of one- and two-story buildings.

The Sausalito cop reached the waterfront, made a broken u-turn and started back up the street toward them, flashing his spotlight from side to side.

"This looks like someplace you wouldn't want to go to by yourself after dark," Harry said.

"Someplace where that creep Karsh would feel right at home," Mulzini said.

* * *

Gina held her arms up to the sky, then rubbed them. Her arms were a cold, wrinkled, fish-belly white from being under water, and her wrists were still seeping blood from cuts she'd made while jabbing at the rope with the broken window glass.

She untied her ankles and tried to stand, but fell and couldn't get up again for a long time.

Every part of her ached as she forced herself to crawl back in the direction of the road. She reached out and planted one hand after another, dragging herself through the mud and water. Every time she tried to stand, her legs collapsed.

Velvety darkness threatened to close in. A voice inside begged her to surrender. But the wind wouldn't let her rest. It whispered, *Up! Get up!*

* * *

Mulzini made a u-turn to follow the sheriff's cruiser; Harry and Vinnie cried out as one, "Stop!"

The Inspector hit the brakes hard and signaled the deputy up ahead by flashing his headlights.

"Over there!" Harry cried out. "That narrow alley on the right. I see something!" He jumped out of the car, Vinnie close behind. They both hit the wet, muddy street running.

"Gina!" Harry screamed, his eyes watering.

She was almost invisible on the ground, covered with mud and curled up in a heap like a pile of discarded garbage. She would have looked dead but for her toes, which kept digging in, trying to push herself forward.

Harry rolled her into his arms. "You're safe, baby." He crooned, rocked her like a lost child. "I've got you, doll. I've got you."

Vinnie wrapped his arms around both of them ... and cried.

Chapter 60

Dehydration, hypothermia, pain, shock, and exhaustion had almost destroyed Gina. She'd been critical for forty-eight hours after Harry and Vinnie found her sprawled in the mud.

The EMTs said she stopped breathing on the way to the hospital and her cardiac rhythm had been dangerously close to shut-down. They'd refused to let Harry ride along – in his state of mind they knew he would have only been another problem to deal with. But Harry was as close as he could get – he and Vinnie were following the ambulance in Inspector Mulzini's car. Sirens, like his heart beat, blasting.

* * *

Gina was just beginning to feel more like her old self. She thought about the last few days in the hospital, sleeping most of the time, complaining about not being allowed to go home the rest of the time.

But no matter how hard she tried, she couldn't remember much of anything about her two days in the ICU. Only flashes of people hovering over her.

Now she was sprawled across the bed in her favorite yellow flannel PJs. She lay next to Harry, who was catnapping.

Poor guy! I've just about done him in ...again.

The doorbell rang and she sat up in bed. She could hear Vinnie talking to someone; she strained to hear.

Taneka! It was Taneka. Within a minute or so, Vinnie led the OB/Gyn charge nurse into the bedroom.

One look at Taneka's face and Gina felt sorry for her. She looked so apologetic and droopy next to the perky bouquet of yellow mums she was holding.

"Hi, Taneka," Harry said

"Hey, how nice of you visit," Gina added.

Her team leader smiled meekly. "I know ... I know. What took me so long?" She looked away, then took in the entire room before bringing her gaze back to return to Gina. "I should have come to see you in the hospital."

"You're here now, that's what counts." Gina pointed at the flowers. "Are those for me?"

"Of course."

Harry reached out for the mums. "I'll go put them in water."

Gina patted the bed next to her. "Sit down."

Taneka sat on the very edge of the bed. Prim, rigid. But then she let the words fly, as though she'd rehearsed them several times.

"I should have believed you, Gina Mazzio, when you told me about Thelma. And if I hadn't left the restaurant that day, none of this," she waved a hand over Gina, "would have happened."

"Taneka, it's not your fault." A gray and white tabby jumped up on the bed, startling them.

"Hi, there, Tuva." Gina wrapped an arm around the cat and brought her up to her chest. "Usually don't see you around when strangers are in the house."

"Tuva? That's an unusual name, especially for a cat."

"She's a rescue. Harry adopted her for me. I named her for a great gal I met in Nevada." Gina was running her fingers back and forth through the tabby's fur – they both laughed at the responsive purr; it sounded like a buzz saw.

"Lying around has given me time to think about everything," Gina said. "Truthfully, Taneka, I think Thelma and Marvin knew they'd never get me alone without your help. I'm sure their plans included getting rid of you, too."

"No!"

"Face it, gal, you, and all those future pregnant women Thelma had planned on getting rid of, you all lucked out."

"I don't think she would have hurt me."

"If she was willing to murder patients because they wanted abortions, and would have murdered me for suspecting her, you really think she would have left you alive as a witness?"

The black woman's face became a pasty gray. "Well, it's all over for her, and they have that husband of hers locked up for her murder and conspiracy to commit murder."

Gina plumped her pillow and sat up taller. "Harry told me Marvin lawyered up, fought the whole thing, and tried to blame it all on an anti-abortion group called The Holy Eye."

"Oh, that's the organization we've been reading about for weeks. They mostly go after Planned Parenthood, but they've been plaguing other women's clinics lately," Taneka said. "They're very pro-active."

"I think that's the one," Gina said. "However, they haven't been able to make a connection between Marvin Karsh's actions and that particular anti-abortion group. The guy in charge claims he threw the Karshes out long ago because of their violent behavior."

"Anyway, Karsh ended up going down with only a whimper," Harry said, coming back into the room with the mums in a cut glass vase. "He pleaded out after he found out the woman he intended to run away with had scheduled an abortion. "As fate would have it, she's scheduled at Ridgewood Woman's Health Clinic."

"Is that true?" Taneka said.

"I swear!"

"How ironic is that?"

"Yeah," Gina said. "Harry says she made some comment about not being up to raising a child on her own, especially the son of a murderer."

* * *

"It was nice of Taneka to drop by," Harry said.

"I'm glad she did."

Harry kissed Gina's wrist, fingered her bandaged wounds gently. "Baby, you've got to stop doing this to me. Some of those cuts were pretty deep ... and that's saying nothing about the rest of your injuries."

"It was the only way I could free myself, Harry. I knew you'd be looking for me, but what if you didn't find me?"

"I know. But you nicked a vein, lost so much blood ... if we hadn't found you when we did..."

"It's not my fault, Harry. Things just happen to me. It's not like I go looking for trouble."

"Maybe it's time for you to just do your job and stop examining everything that's going on all around you."

"I didn't become a nurse to hide in a hole."

"Doll, I need a break," Harry said. "And it's not only me. Vinnie says he's not leaving our apartment until he knows you're safe. Little does he know that may *never* happen."

"I'm really worried about him."

"Well, stop worrying. He's not going anywhere. He's camped out in our spare bedroom ... won't even go back to Helen's."

"I'll talk to him."

"I don't know, Gina. He's obsessed with the idea that Dominick is here in San Francisco and that you need protection."

"Right now, with you here next to me, I feel warm and safe. Not even Dominick could get to me, no matter how hard he tried." She let out a deep sigh. "But my poor little baby brother is still at war with the world ... and everything in it."

"Well, at least he didn't lose his job over walking away to go look for you. No one turned him in, and someone even clocked him out at the end of the day."

"That's super."

"Yeah! Seems there're really a lot of people around here who respect the Mazzio name. Can't imagine why."

"Watch it, buster. We Mazzios are starting to gang up on you."

"Don't I know it! Anyway, there's more good news. Next week, Vinnie starts the evaluation process for his PTSD. He's asked me to go with him."

"You'll go?"

"Of course. I'll be right there every minute."

Gina ran her fingers through his curly hair, rested her head on his shoulder. "What would I do without you? I can't even imagine it."

"I still don't see a ring on that finger that says you're married ... to me."

"Do I need to have a ring?"

He drew her into his arms, buried his head against her shoulder, and whispered, "I need to know you're mine forever, Gina Mazzio." Then he squeezed her so hard her breath caught in her throat. "Do you understand?"

"I do, Harry. I really do."

# # #

About the Authors

Bette Golden Lamb, a feisty ex-Bronxite, writes crime novels and plays with clay. Her sculptures, paintings, and other artistic creations appear in international exhibitions, Western galleries, and various retail outlets. She also hangs out in her garden with 50+ rose bushes, or sneaks out to movies with her collaborator when she should be writing. Being an RN is a huge clue as to why she writes medical thrillers.

J. J. Lamb intended to become an aeronautical engineer and pilot, but was seduced by journalism. An AP career was interrupted by the Army, which gave him a *Top Secret* clearance; a locked room with table, chair, and typewriter; and the time to write short stories. A paperback PI series followed, then collaboration with Bette. *No Pat Hands,* in his Zach Rolfe III PI series, was nominated for a 2014 Shamus Award from Private Eye Writers of America.

The Lambs, who live in Northern California, have co-authored five medical thrillers - *Bone Dry, Sisters in Silence, Sin & Bone, Bone Pit* and *Bone of Contention* - and a suspense-adventure-romance novel, *Heir Today.* They are members of Mystery Writers of America, Sisters in Crime, and International Thriller Writers.

www.twoblacksheep.us